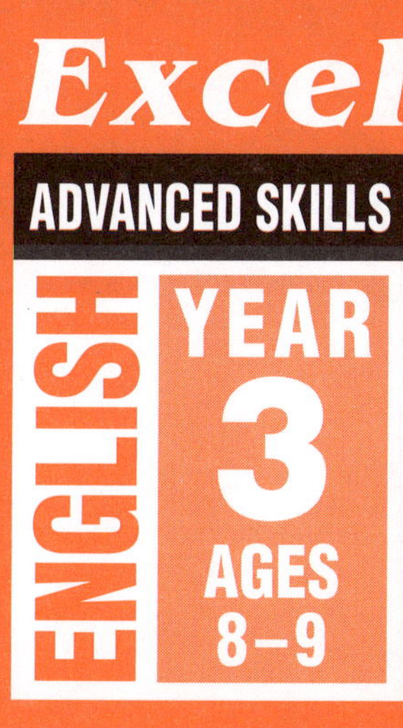

SPELLING AND VOCABULARY WORKBOOK

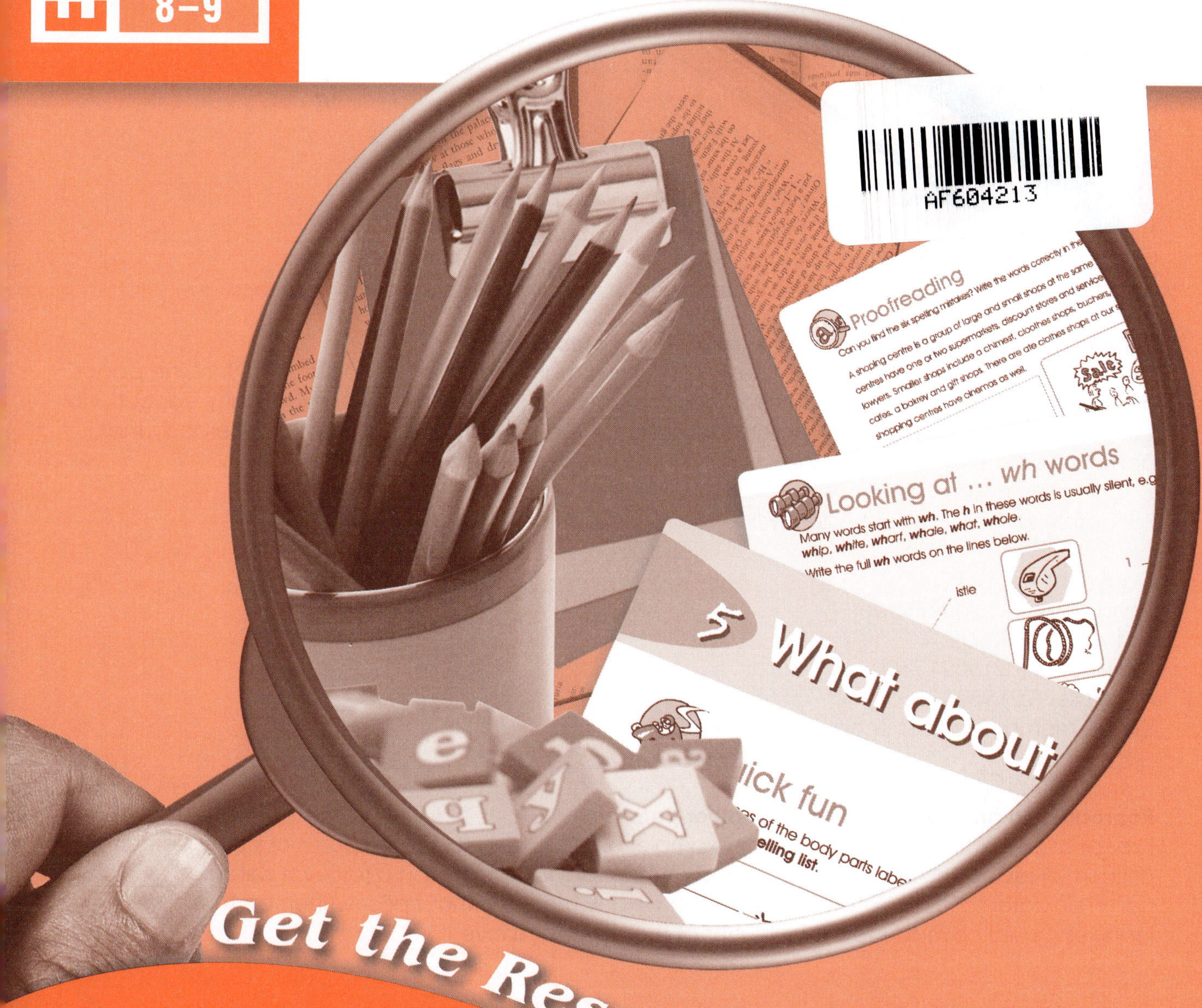

Get the Results You Want!

PASCAL PRESS

Alan Horsfield &
Wendy-Grace Williams

Reprinted 2008, 2009, 2011, 2012, 2013, 2015, 2016 (twice), 2017, 2019, 2020, 2022, 2023

ISBN 978 1 74125 260 6

Pascal Press
PO Box 250
Glebe NSW 2037
(02) 9198 1748
www.pascalpress.com.au

Publisher: Vivienne Joannou
Series developer: Kristine Brown
Project editor: Mark Dixon
Edited by Mark Dixon
Reviewed by Carolyn Lain and Claire Balaam
Typeset by Grizzly Graphics (Leanne Richters)
Cover and page design by DiZign Pty Ltd
Printed by Vivar Printing/Green Giant Press

Contents

Map of the book . . . . . Inside front cover
To the student iv

1 Let's go shopping 2
2 Lend a hand 8
3 A walk in the park 14
4 Once upon a time 20
5 What about me? 26
Review 1: Tests 1–4 32

6 On the farm 36
7 Travelling on 42
8 Be a sport 48
9 To the zoo 54
10 Our world 60
Review 2: Tests 1–4 66

11 What's your number? 70
12 Water, water 76
13 What did you say? 82
14 For the birds 88
15 It's about time 94
Review 3: Tests 1–4 100

Word list 104
Answers 108

To the student

Winnie the Pooh thought he was a good speller. It was just that some of the letters got out of order! The problem is that to be a good speller, all letters have to be in the correct order.

You can learn to be a good speller. There are rules for spelling words and there are spelling patterns that match sound patterns. This book will show you some of those patterns and teach you some of those rules. It will even teach you clever tricks to help you remember long words and words that don't fit the rules.

You will need a dictionary (*The Macquarie Junior Dictionary* if possible) and a sharp pencil. You will also need a quiet place to work with good light so you don't strain your eyes. You will be able to do the exercises in this book all by yourself if you have all those things.

It will also be a big help if you have an adult or big brother or sister to hear you spell the words once you think you know them. When you spell a word aloud to someone else, it stays in your brain much longer than if you just spell it to yourself.

You can't write well without good spelling. When you have finished this book, you will be well on the way to becoming a good writer.

You'll also find fun puzzles using the words from each unit. There are crosswords, wordsearches and sometimes anagrams (rearranging the letters of one word to make a new word) and palindromes (words that can be spelled forwards or backwards!). There are jokes and riddles at the end of each unit that use the words you are learning.

I hope you enjoy working through the book. Good luck and have fun!

LOOK-SAY-COVER-WRITE-CHECK method

The best way to learn new spellings is the **LOOK-SAY-COVER-WRITE-CHECK** method.

- **LOOK** hard at the word.

  Think about the meaning. If you don't know the meaning, find it out.

  Think about patterns in the word. Does it follow the same pattern as other words you know? Are there any parts that don't follow the usual pattern?

  Underline the difficult letters that are especially hard to remember.

  Think about the look of the word. Take a picture of it mentally.

- **SAY** the word out loud, thinking about how it breaks up into syllables.

  Close your eyes and picture it in your mind while you say it. Write it in the air if you want to.

- **COVER** the word up and **WRITE** it without looking back.

- **CHECK** it.

  If you get it right, write it once more.

  If you get it wrong, do the **LOOK-SAY-COVER-WRITE-CHECK** method again until you get it right.

1 Let's go shopping

Quick fun

Here are some shopping words.

bakery	bank
food	supermarket
shop	books

Can you unscramble these shopping words using the list above?

1. ABKN ______________________
2. RYEBAK ______________________
3. DOFO ______________________
4. BOKOS ______________________
5. OPHS ______________________
6. MEERKATRSUP ______________________

Topic spelling list

Use the **LOOK-SAY-COVER-WRITE-CHECK** strategy to learn these words.

supermarket	shopping	fruit
clothes	bank	chemist
shop	books	stamps
food	socks	milk
bakery	shoes	meat
butcher	newspaper	cash

Use this space to write out your topic words the first time. Use your own paper for extra practice.

____

Rewrite here those you had most trouble with.

____

Spelling strategy

Learning new words

To learn new words—or practise words you need to remember—a useful idea is the LOOK, SAY, COVER, WRITE, CHECK method. (You can check this out on page 1 at the beginning of this book.)

Choose six of the most challenging words you would like to learn to spell from the **Topic spelling list** above. Write your words in the grid below.

	LOOK, SAY	COVER	WRITE	CHECK
1				
2				
3				
4				
5				
6				

Put a cross next to the words that are spelt incorrectly and write the correct spelling next to each word.

1. bakry ______________________
2. butcher ______________________
3. shose ______________________
4. mete ______________________

Fill in the gaps

Choose words from the **Topic spelling list** to complete these sentences.

1. Whenever we go shopping, we usually have to visit the ____________________ first to withdraw some ____________________ from the automatic teller machine (ATM).
2. When I go to the shopping centre, I have favourite ____________________ I like to visit.
3. At the supermarket we buy fresh ____________________ and vegetables.
4. At the butcher we buy ____________________ and pet food.
5. We go to the Post Office to buy ____________________.
6. Every day, Dad goes to the paper shop to buy a ____________________.
7. The word ____________________ from the **Topic spelling list** rhymes with *clocks*.

Tricky words

The words ***bought*** and ***brought*** sound much the same but are easily confused.

Word	Meaning	Example
bought	Think of *buy*. We use it after making our purchase.	*I **bought** a book and a newspaper at the shopping centre.*
brought	Think of *bring*. We use it after we have delivered something.	*Kate **brought** her bag to school but left her books at home.*

Complete the sentences below with the correct word (*bought* or *brought*).

1. Toby ________________ his new bat and Len ________________ an old ball to play with.
2. 'Who ________________ the dog to school?' asked the teacher.
3. I ________________ a custard tart for $1.50.
4. When Dad ________________ his new car he was all smiles.
5. We all ________________ notes to school for the trip to the bakery.

Looking at … vowels and consonants

Vowels are ***a***, ***e***, ***i***, ***o*** and ***u***. Say them softly. All the other letters are **consonants**.

Choose 10 words from the **Topic spelling list**. Write one word in each box below. Use a red pen for the vowels and a green pen for the consonants, e.g. in *supermarket*: the ***u***, ***e***, ***a***, ***e*** would be written in red and the ***s***, ***p***, ***r***, ***m***, ***r***, ***k***, and ***t*** would be written in green.

	Write the word here	Now write it using different colours
1		
2		
3		
4		
5		
6		
7		
8		
9		
10		

Proofreading

Can you find the six spelling mistakes? Write the words correctly in the box below.

A shoping centre is a group of large and small shops at the same spot. Most shopping centres have one or two supermarkets, discount stores and services such as doctors and lawyers. Smaller shops include a chimest, cloothes shops, buchers, shoe shops, hairdressers, cafes, a bakrey and gift shops. There are ate clothes shops at our shopping centre. Some shopping centres have cinemas as well.

Vocabulary power

Many words in English are made up from two smaller words. The new words are called **compound words**, e.g. ***super*** + ***market*** = ***supermarket***.
Make the two short words into one long compound word.

1. hair + dresser = ______________________
2. news + papers = ______________________
3. suit + case = ______________________
4. class + room = ______________________
5. news + agent = ______________________
6. green + grocer = ______________________
7. wheel + chair = ______________________
8. hay + stack = ______________________
9. scare + crow = ______________________
10. bush + fire = ______________________

Read and learn

Work out the meanings of the words in **bold** by using the context (the meaning of the surrounding words).

Names of shops change over the years. Names such as *greengrocer* and *milk bar* are becoming old fashioned because most shops now sell a greater range of **products**. Convenience stores, once called 'one-stop-shops', were one of the first to move into **providing** a wider range of products. It was **convenient** for customers to **purchase** most of what they needed from the one store. 'Cash and carry' was a name given to such stores, but this name is **seldom** used now, as many people use credit cards instead of cash! Barbers have become hairdressers, health food stores are popping up in every suburb and town, and tobacconists have almost disappeared.

Circle the answers **a**, **b** or **c** that mean almost the same as the words in **bold** above.

1 products	**a** goods	**b** food	**c** makes
2 providing	**a** proving	**b** supplying	**c** using
3 convenient	**a** handy	**b** small	**c** neat
4 purchase	**a** get	**b** take	**c** buy
5 seldom	**a** usually	**b** rarely	**c** never

Puzzle

Can you find these words in the wordsearch below?

B	A	K	E	R	Y	N	C	O	C
U	A	E	A	S	Z	Y	L	D	P
T	R	G	I	X	S	H	O	E	S
C	H	E	M	I	S	T	T	B	O
H	J	G	M	I	L	F	H	O	C
E	F	F	E	B	C	O	E	O	K
R	T	B	L	D	B	O	S	K	S
U	H	B	R	E	A	D	G	S	Q
F	R	U	I	T	N	W	I	J	X
V	K	M	I	L	K	C	A	S	H

BAKERY
BANK
BUTCHER
BOOKS
BREAD
CASH
CHEMIST
CLOTHES
FOOD
FRUIT
MILK
SHOES
SOCKS

Find one word from the **Topic spelling list** connected with the following things.

1 apples, lemons, pears, plums, cherries ____________________

2 chops, sausages, mince, steak, pork ____________________

Your turn to write

You are in a crowded shopping centre with your younger brother or sister. You turn around and he/she has disappeared. You have to find your brother or sister quickly. Tell how you rush from shop to shop, searching. Where do you find him/her? You can make your story amusing or exciting. At the end of your story, draw a picture.

Revise and edit your work when you finish. Check all punctuation and spelling. You may have to use a dictionary to help you.

When you are happy with your story, you can make a published copy for your teacher, parent or friend. You could publish it on a computer.

Lost in the supermarket

Reading for fun

Sally went to the pet shop at the shopping mall. 'Do you have any bird seed?' she asked the owner.

The owner said he sold bird seed. 'What sort of birds do you have?' he asked.

Sally replied, 'Oh, I don't have any yet. I just want to grow some.'

Waiter, waiter! Do you have soup on the menu in this cafe?
No Sir, I wiped it all off!

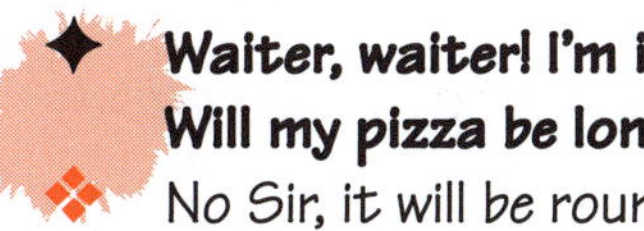

Waiter, waiter! I'm in a hurry. Will my pizza be long?
No Sir, it will be round!

☞Answers on page 108

2 Lend a hand

Quick fun

How many words of three or more letters can you make from the following table in three minutes? You can only use each letter once.

Can you get the eight-letter word? Clue: it's an entertainer.

M	I	N	U
S	C	A	I

Topic spelling list

Use the **LOOK-SAY-COVER-WRITE-CHECK** strategy to learn these words.

nurse	artist	doctor
actor	builder	policeman
driver	friend	banker
hairdresser	musician	barber
plumber	parents	teacher
dentist	baker	fireman

Use this space to write out your topic words the first time. Use your own paper for extra practice.

Rewrite here those you had most trouble with.

Spelling strategy

Word shapes

Can you see what the word looks like in your head? Think of the word ***dog***. What shape is the word? What shape are the letters? Which letters go above or below the line? This strategy can help you remember how to spell words.

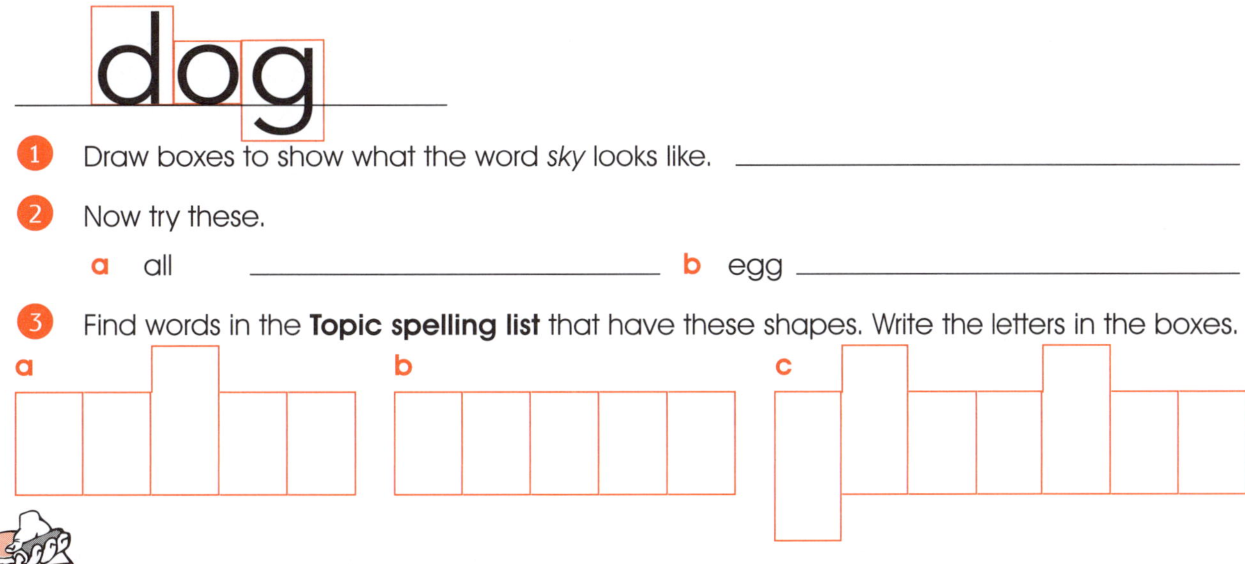

1 Draw boxes to show what the word *sky* looks like. ______________________

2 Now try these.

a all ______________________ b egg ______________________

3 Find words in the **Topic spelling list** that have these shapes. Write the letters in the boxes.

a

b

c

Fill in the gaps

1 Can you find words in the **Topic spelling list** for the person who does these things? There may be more than one answer. This person …

a works in hospitals ______________ b puts out fires ______________

c cuts hair ______________ d is a mother or father ______________

e plays in a band ______________ f works in a school ______________

g looks after teeth ______________ h keeps us safe ______________

i can be seen on stage ______________

2 Who are these people?

a

b

c

d

e

______________ ______________ ______________ ______________ ______________

3. The picture below shows the inside of a building. What building is it?

____

4. The person in the picture below is called a …

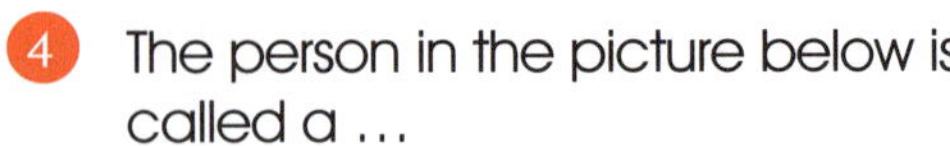

____

Tricky words

The words ***blew*** and ***blue*** sound the same but have different spellings. Words that sound the same but have different spellings are called **homophones.**

Word	Meaning	Example
blew	air that has moved	*Mother **blew** up the balloons for the party.*
blue	one of the three primary colours	*Some of the balloons were as **blue** as the sky.*

Complete the sentences below with the correct word (*blew* or *blue*).

1. The wind ______________ all night long!
2. Kirsty ______________ the candles out on her birthday cake.
3. The water in the pool was ______________.
4. Some girls have ______________ eyes.

Vocabulary power

For some words, adding ***in*** to the start (a **prefix**) makes a word into its opposite, e.g.

correct → ***in**correct* (not correct)
expensive → ***in**expensive* (not expensive)

Reminder
The prefix *-in* can simply mean 'being in something', such as *inland*, *inmate* and *inside*.

Using the prefix ***in-***, write the **opposite** of the following words.

1. visible ______________
2. direct ______________
3. sane ______________
4. complete ______________
5. human ______________

Looking at ... plurals: adding s

Many words change from one item to more than one simply by adding an **s**, e.g.

one school → *six school**s***
one hat → *many hat**s***
a newspaper → *seven newspaper**s***

Now it's your turn. Change these singular words into plurals.

One	More than one	One	More than one
1 cat		2 seat	
3 book		4 baker	
5 house		6 nurse	
7 actor		8 plumber	

Proofreading

Dad made a list before going to the shops. Find the six spelling mistakes and write them correctly in the box below.

Dad's shoping list and things to do

Make a time for haircut
with barbar.
Butcher: chops and sausages.
Supermarket: melk, warter,
cordial, tea, friut
Bank: $250 cash from ATM
Baker: 6 BBQ buns, sliced bread
Post Office: stampes, newspaper

Read and learn

Work out the meanings of the words in **bold** by using the context.

The stage play of

Treasure Island

Starring Graham Hunt and a band of pirates!
Opening Night Friday 5 June

COMING SOON

BOOK NOW!

'Right, hold it there! That was much better!' **reported** Margaret Walton, the play's director, from a front row seat in the Town Hall. A few stagehands were spread **sparsely** throughout other seats.

The actors on stage relaxed. Graham Hunt, who was playing Long John Silver, rubbed his hand through Jamie's hair. 'Not bad for a beginner,' he **commended**.

Jamie, playing Jim Hawkins, knew how much the play depended upon him. The dress **rehearsal** was the next night and the play **opened** on Friday night. He was getting **butterflies**.

Circle the answers **a**, **b** or **c** that mean almost the same as the words in **bold** above.

		a	b	c
1	reported	a advised	b ordered	c studied
2	sparsely	a quietly	b thinly	c happily
3	commended	a explained	b praised	c noticed
4	rehearsal	a repeat	b take	c practice
5	opened	a acted	b started	c uncovered
6	butterflies	a insects	b airborne	c nervous

Puzzle

Using the words in the box, unscramble the words below. Write them on the lines provided.

plumber baker dentist nurse policeman doctor

1

a

____

b

D	S	T
N	E	I
	T	

____

c
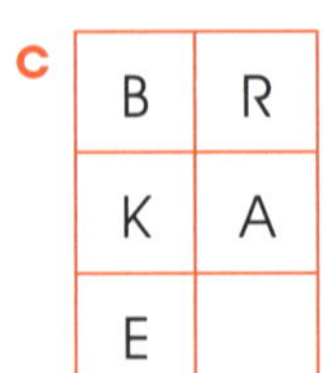

____

d

P	E	M
B	U	R
	L	

____

e

N
S
U
R
E

____

f

M	A	N
P	C	E
L	I	O

____

2 Can you do these without any help? They are all words from the **Topic spelling list**.

a

R	F
D	E
I	N

b

U	I	I
M	C	N
S	A	

c

T	S
R	A
I	T

d

F	I	M
E	N	A
	R	

e

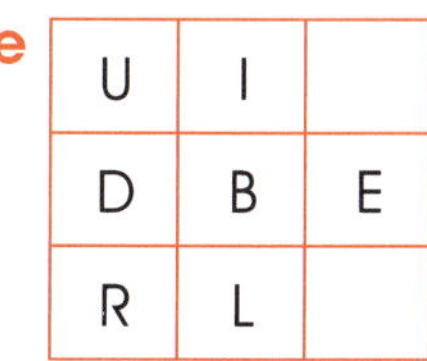

U	I	
D	B	E
R	L	

a ______ b ______ c ______ d ______ e ______

Your turn to write

There has been a robbery. You were standing on the footpath when the thief came out of a shop and ducked down a side lane. Write a short report to tell what people who worked nearby did.

At the end of your story, draw a picture. Show some action in your picture. Revise and edit your work when you finish. Check all punctuation and spelling. You may have to use a dictionary to help you.

When you are happy with your story, you can make a published copy for your teacher, parent or friend. You could publish it on a computer.

Supermarket robbery

____

____

____

____

____

____

____

____

____

Reading for fun

While waiting for a train, my friend started a conversation with another traveller.

'I have a great teacher joke. Would you like to hear it?' she asked.

'First, I should warn you that I am a teacher,' the other traveller replied.

'No problem. I promise to tell it *really* slow!'

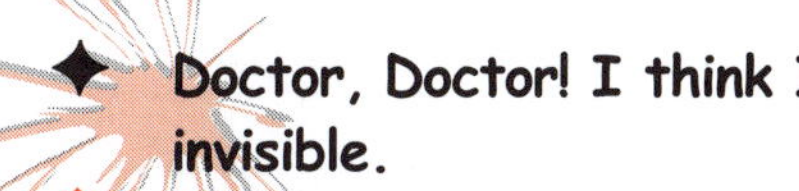

Doctor, Doctor! I think I'm invisible.

Come back later, I can't see you now!

Doctor, Doctor! I'm losing my memory.

When did that happen?

When did what happen?

Answers on page 108

3 A walk in the park

Quick fun

Did you know if you spell some words backwards, you get another word! e.g.

but → *tub* *step* → *pets* *wolf* → *flow* *stink* → *knits*

What do the following words become when spelled backwards?

1 ________ 2 ________ 3 ________ 4 ________

The words below are from the **Topic spelling list** but they are written backwards. What are they?

5 cisum ________ 6 efac ________

7 ekal ________ 8 krab ________

Topic spelling list

Use the **LOOK-SAY-COVER-WRITE-CHECK** strategy to learn these words.

dogs	sport	picnic
playing	grass	cafe
lake	birds	music
branches	kiosk	insects
bark	path	seats
leaves	green	visitors

Use this space to write out your topic words the first time. Use your own paper for extra practice.

Rewrite here those you had most trouble with.

Spelling strategy

Letter patterns: *ea* words

When ***e*** and ***a*** are next to each other in a word, the ***e*** comes before the ***a***.

Using this trick will help you remember how to spell the word. Look out for words that follow this pattern.

eat	**ea**r	**ea**ch	**ea**rn	**ea**st
l**ea**ves	l**ea**n	l**ea**f	l**ea**d	
s**ea**ts	s**ea**t	s**ea**shore	s**ea**l	

1 How many words do you know that rhyme with *s**ea**t* and have **ea** in them? Write your words here. The first letters have been done for you.

a s ______ **b** h ______ **c** tr ______ **d** wh ______

e b ______ **f** n ______ **g** m ______ **g** rep ______

2 What is the missing word?

North, south, ______ and west.

Fill in the gaps

Complete the text using words from the box.

music	seats	birds	branches	insects	tree
leaves	visitors	lake	flowers	park	dogs

The band played (1) ______ by the kiosk while many (2) ______ admired the trees and the (3) ______. Several people were walking their (4) ______ through the park enjoying the fresh air. People were sitting on (5) ______ near the (6) ______ feeding the ducks and other (7) ______. One family was having a picnic near the oak (8) ______. The wind blew (9) ______ from its (10) ______. Crickets and other (11) ______ were chirping happily. It was peaceful at the (12) ______.

Tricky words

The words ***brake*** and ***break*** sound the same but have different spellings. These kinds of words are called **homophones**.

Word	Meaning	Example
brake	1 slow down	You need to ***brake*** at traffic lights.
	2 a device to slow something down	*The **brake** on my bike was fixed.*
break	1 get damaged, often leaving an object in pieces	*Did Jane **break** the cup when she dropped it?*
	2 a short gap between events	There's a ten-minute ***break*** soon.

Complete the sentences with the correct word (*brake* or *break*).

1. Tom will ________________ the chair if he stands on it.
2. There is a ten-minute ________________ between the lessons.
3. When the car stopped, Dad pulled on the hand________________.
4. Did Lisa ________________ the race record?
5. Most cars have a hand________________ and a foot________________.
6. Did the old car ________________ down on the way to the park?

Circle the correct word in this sentence.

7. If we have a *(break / brake)* for lunch, we won't be able to finish.

Looking at … plurals: adding es *to* words ending in *ch* and *sh*

Some words change from one item to more than one by adding **es**. To form the plural, you must add ***es*** to words that end in ***ch*** or ***sh***.

ch	one wat**ch**	two watch**es**	sh	one da**sh**	two dash**es**

Now try these.

1 one branch	two
2 one splash	two
3 one bunch	two
4 one crash	two
5 one lunch	two
6 one patch	two

Proofreading

1 Find five spelling mistakes and write them correctly in the box below.

Brad took his kite to the park. He ran along the parth, dragging his kite, but it didn't fly. He looked for another place. The oval was covered in soft gras and there were only to trees. The wind was getting stronger. He'd give it a go.

He let out more string. A sudden gust of wind ripped the kite from his hands. It flew above the kiosk and landed among the laeves and branchs of an old tree.

2 Greg wrote labels for his pictures. Put a cross near the labels he misspelled and write the correct word underneath each picture.

a 
dogs ____

b 
brids ____

c 
insecks ____

d 
picnick ____

e 
cafe ____

Vocabulary power

Words can have more than one meaning. Let's look at the word ***bark***. It can mean:

1 the sound a dog makes
2 the outer 'skin' of a tree.

Can you find the words from the **Topic Spelling list** that have all the following meanings?

1
- a a place to leave many cars
- b a public grassy place for sport or relaxing
- c stop and leave a car

The word is ________________.

2
- a something to sit on
- b part of clothing that covers a person's backside
- c the flat part of a chair

The word is ________________.

3
- a a colour
- b not ripe
- c envious or jealous

The word is ________________.

Read and learn

Use the context clues to work out the meanings of the words in **bold**.

The word *trunk* is unusual because it has **various** meanings. For example, the main woody stem of a tree is called its *trunk*, but the word is also the name given to the rear storage **compartment** of a car, a travelling box or case, the long nose of an elephant, and the human torso (that is, the upper part of the human body **excluding** the head and limbs). *Trunks* is a **dated** word for men's swimming costumes. *Trunk* also has several other unusual meanings. If you used your computer, could you **discover** what they are?

Circle the answers **a**, **b** or **c** that mean almost the same as the words in **bold** above.

1	various	**a**	strange	**b**	special	**c**	several
2	compartment	**a**	hole	**b**	section	**c**	opening
3	excluding	**a**	apart from	**b**	praised	**c**	noticed
4	dated	**a**	forgotten	**b**	old-fashioned	**c**	used
5	discover	**a**	learn	**b**	reveal	**c**	investigate

Puzzle

Can you match the scrambled words on the left to the words on the right? Draw lines.

kael	trunk
kkois	bark
ranchbes	grass
nurtk	leaves
eatss	visitors
rassg	path
aeelvs	kiosk
karb	seats
rostsiiv	lake
hapt	branches

Your turn to write

Write about an experience you have had in a park. Make it a factual recount of things that have really happened to you. What happened first? What happened next? What happened at the end? These events must be true.

At the end of your recount, draw a picture of one thing you did. Revise and edit your work when you finish. Check all punctuation and spelling. You may have to use a dictionary to help you.

When you are happy with your work, you can make a published copy for your teacher, parent or friend. You could publish it on a computer.

Park experience

____

____

____

____

____

____

____

____

____

____

____

____

Reading for fun

Josie met her friend in the park. She noticed her friend was walking two new dogs, so she asked what their names were.
The friend said that one was named Rolex and one was named Seiko.
Josie said, 'Whoever heard of someone naming dogs something like that?'
The friend replied, 'What else are you going to name watchdogs?'

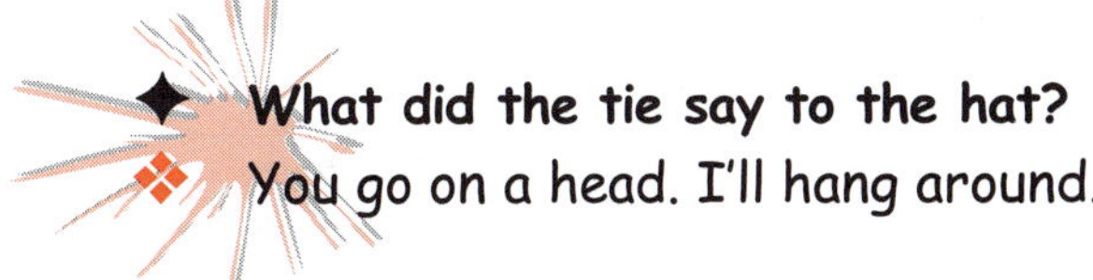

What did the tie say to the hat?
You go on a head. I'll hang around.

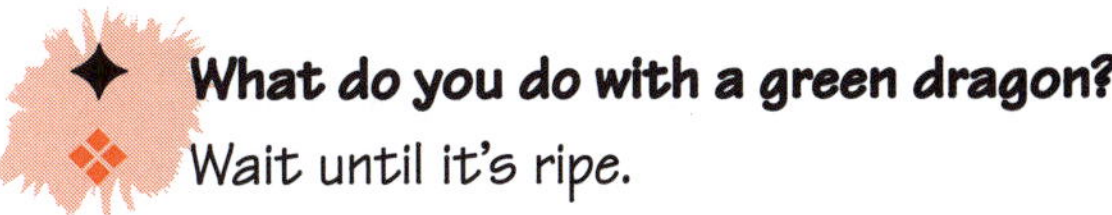

What do you do with a green dragon?
Wait until it's ripe.

☞Answers on page 109

4 Once upon a time

Quick fun

1 Find words from the **Topic spelling list** that match the definitions below. The first one has been done for you.

a a daughter of a king and queen	princess
b a huge person	
c a person who can cast magic spells	
d a fairy-like creature	
e a spirit of a person who has died	
f a very small person with wings	

2 If I start my story with *Once upon a time*, what sort of story will it be?

___

Topic spelling list

Use the **LOOK-SAY-COVER-WRITE-CHECK** strategy to learn these words.

once	fairy	happily
troll	dwarf	ugly
giant	ghost	witch
wizard	tale	elf
gnome	magician	told
princess	pixie	magic

Use this space to write out your topic words the first time. Use your own paper for extra practice.

Rewrite here those you had most trouble with.

Spelling strategy

Letter patterns: endings

Rhyming words often have endings that have the same spelling, e.g. s***ell*** and w***ell*** rhyme and both end with ***ell***.

Using letter patterns at the end of words will help you remember how to spell the word. Can you find six more ***ell*** words to go with these?

sp**ell** w**ell** sh**ell** c**ell**

__________________ __________________

__________________ __________________

__________________ __________________

Tongue twister

Can you say this sentence quickly three times?

Mary sells seashells on the sea shore and the sea shells she sells come off the sea shore.

Fill in the gaps

Complete the text using the words from the box.

happily	princess	king	queen	wood
giant	love	time	prince	after

'Once upon a (1) ______________' (that's how all fairy tales begin), there lived a (2) ______________ and queen and a very unhappy princess. The (3) ______________ was unhappy because she had not yet met her handsome (4) ______________. Her mother, the (5) ______________, had sent her away to Princess Finishing School—but it was only for princesses. There was not a prince to be seen. One day she decided to sneak away and go for a walk in the wood. In the (6) ______________ she came across a knight slaying a (7) ______________. Well, you should be able to guess the rest of the story. She immediately fell in (8) ______________ with him, got married and they lived (9) ______________ ever (10) ______________—and so they should!

Tricky words

The words ***buy*** and ***by*** sound the same but have different spellings. Words that sound the same but have different spellings are called **homophones**.

Word	Meaning	Example
buy	purchase something using money	*Julie wanted to* ***buy*** *a new bicycle.*
by	1 beside, near to or close	*Justin put his bike* ***by*** *the front gate.*
	2 showing who has done something	*This book was written* ***by*** *Charles Dickens.*
	3 showing how something is done	*Doug cleaned out the drain* ***by*** *hand.*

Complete the sentences with the correct word (*buy* or *by*).

1. 'Can you ______________ that book for me?' asked Bev.
2. A bird just flew ______________ our window.
3. I bought a sample bag at the show. What did you ______________?
4. I finished my homework ______________ the light of a candle.
5. ______________ the time we get home I will be hungry.
6. This photo was taken ______________ my brother.

Looking at … plurals: words ending in *f*

Some words are made into plurals by changing the final ***f*** into ***v*** and adding **es**, e.g.

*el**f*** → *el**ves***   *dwar**f*** → *dwar**ves***

Now it's your turn. Change the following singular words into plurals.

Singular (one)	Plural (more than one)
1 wharf	
2 hoof	
3 calf	
4 half	
5 leaf	
6 scarf	

We also change ***f*** into ***v*** when some words change from nouns to verbs, e.g.

*belie**f*** → *belie**ve***   *relie**f*** → *relie**ve***

Proofreading

Find six spelling mistakes and write them correctly in the box below.

A wicked wich was dressed up as a kindly old lady. She gave Snow White a delicious red apple. Snow White was both a little thirsty and hungry. She happiley bit into the apple. Unfortunately, she only eight one mouthful before she fell to the gras, fast asleep. The majic was so strong that Snow White could stay asleep forever. Luckily for Snow White, a handsome prints came along and kissed her—and she woke up!

Vocabulary power

Adjectives make your writing more interesting. Adjectives describe nouns, e.g. ***red*** *apple*, ***seven*** *dwarves*, ***young*** *prince*, ***happy*** *smile*.

Write an adjective for each of these words in the spaces below.

1 ______________________ wizard
2 ______________________ witch
3 ______________________ ghost
4 ______________________ giant
5 ______________________ leaf
6 ______________________ bird

Now choose a word that might describe each of the following adjectives.

7 huge ______________________
8 pretty ______________________

Read and learn

Use the context clues to work out the meanings of the words in **bold**.

For centuries authors have written stories about fairies, which often live at the bottom of our gardens. They are **generally** invisible to human beings, and mostly do good **deeds**. Unfortunately some fairies are naughty, and a few, like Rumpelstiltskin, are cruel and **spiteful**. Two famous fairies are the Tooth Fairy, who **exchanges** baby teeth for money, and the Sandman, who sprinkles fairy dust in children's eyes to make them sleep.

Another 'baddie' is the bogeyman, an evil fairy which carries off children who are naughty. Some parents use

the **expression**, 'You'd better behave or the bogeyman will get you!' Do you believe them?

Circle the answers a, b or c that mean almost the same as the words in **bold** above.

1. generally — a almost — b usually — c nearly
2. deeds — a works — b papers — c turns
3. spiteful — a spitting — b naughty — c nasty
4. exchanges — a sells — b buys — c swaps
5. expression — a noise — b saying — c voice

Puzzle

Look at this sentence.

*Th**e** **e**l**f** **f**ough**t** **t**e**n** **n**e**w** **w**icke**d** **d**warves.*

Each new word starts with the last letter of the word that comes before it, e.g.
*Th***e** ends with **e** and **e***lf* starts with **e**.

Write two sentences like this that use one (or more) of the words from the **Topic spelling list**.

1. Start with *Few*. You can use plurals if it helps.

   Few ______________________________

   ____

2. Now try *Big*.

   Big ______________________________

   ____

Your turn to write

Start to rewrite *Goldilocks and the Three Bears* but change Goldilocks to a boy and the bears to crocodiles living in a swamp. Let your imagination run free. Start with *Once upon a time* …

If you know a better fairy tale, you can use that, but make sure you change it—a lot! At the end of your tale, draw a picture of your story. Revise and edit your work when you finish. Check all punctuation and spelling. You may have to use a dictionary to help you.

When you are happy with your story, you can make a published copy for your teacher, parents or friends. You could publish it on a computer.

Fairy tale

Reading for fun

A giant is overweight. His doctor suggests a diet. 'I want you to eat normally for two days, then skip a day. Do that for two weeks. The next time I see you, you'll have lost at least 5 kilograms.'

When the giant returns, he has lost nearly 10 kilograms.

'That's amazing!' the doctor says. 'Did you follow my instructions?'

The giant nods. 'I thought I was going to drop dead that third day.'

'From hunger, you mean?' asked the doctor.

'No, from skipping.'

✦ **There are many castles in the world, but who is strong enough to move one?**

❖ A chess player!

✦ ***What do you call a smelly fairy?***

❖ Stinkerbell.

☞Answers on page 109

5 What about me?

Quick fun

Write the names of the body parts labelled below. The words are from the **Topic spelling list**.

Use this space to write out your topic words the first time. Use your own paper for extra practice.

Rewrite here those you had most trouble with.

Topic spelling list

Use the **LOOK-SAY-COVER-WRITE-CHECK** strategy to learn these words.

ankle	brain	chest
mouth	nerve	finger
hair	health	knuckle
bone	calf	neck
energy	feet	smile
hips	heart	eyes

Spelling strategy

Letter patterns: revising new words

Choose five of the most challenging words you would like to learn to spell from the **Topic spelling list**. Write your words in the table below.

	LOOK, SAY	COVER	WRITE	CHECK
1				
2				
3				
4				
5				
6				

Fill in the gaps

Select words from the list below to complete the conversation.

bone hair hip heart energy health medicine nerves

" I have some good news and some bad news for you, Mr Boneshaker. Your skin is fine but you are going bald. You are losing your 1 ______________________.

Your 2 ______________________ isn't what it once was and you must try not to overdo it. Most people your age have had at least one broken 3 ______________________. Many people your age have a 4 ______________________ problem but it is OK to walk the dog.

I'll prescribe some 5 ______________________ for your loss of 6 ______________________ and something for your 7 ______________________ but I suggest you don't go on another skiing holiday for a while.

Most people of 93 would be worried about their 8 ______________________ and safety! "

Tricky words

The words ***dear*** and ***deer*** sound the same but have different spellings. Words that sound the same but have different spellings are called **homophones**.

Word	Meaning	Example
dear	1 expensive, high in price	*That ring is too* ***dear****.*
	2 a term for affection; loved	*You are very* ***dear*** *to me.*
deer	a large mammal (animal)	*The* ***deer*** *was covered in snow.*

Complete the following sentences with the correct word (*dear* or *deer*).

1. 'Ten dollars for an ice cream? That's ____________________!' exclaimed Jane.
2. A ____________________ with a red nose pulled a sleigh.
3. My sister is ____________________ to me. She stayed with me during my illness.
4. What is this animal? It's a ____________________.

Looking at … plurals: adding es to words ending in *s*, *x* or *z*

Some words change from one item to more than one by adding **es**. You add **es** to words that end in ***s***, ***x*** or ***z***.

s	one gla**ss**	two glass**es**
x	one fo**x**	two fox**es**
z	one qui**z**	two quizz**es**

1. Now try the following words.

a one box	two
b one class	two
c one cake mix	two cake
d one buzz	two
e one school bus	two school
f pass	two

2. **a** While playing cricket, Jan hit one six but Tara hit three ____________________.

   b Tom only bowled one full toss and Evan bowled three full ____________________.

Proofreading

Find seven spelling mistakes and write them correctly in the box below.

Your heart is a powerful pump. It has lots of jobs two do each day with no time off for sleep or play. It sits in the middle of your chess behind a cage of boans called the ribcage. From here it pumps blood to all parts of your body: head, neck, nuckles, fingeres, ankles and feet.

For good health, you should look after your hart by exercising and eating the write foods.

Vocabulary power

Over the years, many parts of our body have been given new meanings.

Let's use ***finger*** as the starting point. What do you really mean by *fingers crossed*? It could just mean 'one finger across another', but for some people it could also mean 'being honest' or 'hoping for good luck'.

What do the following terms mean? Write a short explanation for each. (You could ask an adult for help, or you could check a dictionary or the Internet.)

1. fingerling ______________________
2. finger food ______________________
3. wouldn't lift a finger to help ______________________
4. at my fingertips ______________________
5. slipped through my fingers ______________________
6. butterfingers ______________________

Signs like this are often called finger posts. They point the way just like someone pointing.

Read and learn

Let's learn some new vocabulary!

The **heart** is a muscular organ that pumps blood around the human body. It was once regarded as the centre of all emotion. That's why we have words such as *heartbreak*, *heartache*, *heartless* and *heartrending*.

1. Where would I find the Queen of Hearts? ______________________________

2. When is a person brokenhearted? ______________________________

____

Can you think of any other words that begin with or include the word *heart*?

Puzzle

An **anagram** is a new word that uses all the letters of another word, e.g.
rat → *art, tar*   *rate* → *tear*
Find anagrams for the following words from words used in this unit.

1. dare ______________________________
2. ship ______________________________
3. reed ______________________________
4. fete ______________________________
5. earth ______________________________
6. limes ______________________________
7. hater ______________________________
8. never ______________________________

Your turn to write

You don't feel well. Write five excuses for why you can't go to school today. Use some of the words from the **Topic spelling list**. You can make it humorous if you like. What do you think your parents would say about your best excuse?

At the end of your excuses, draw a picture of the head and shoulders of you and your mum or dad. Write what you would say in your speech bubble and what your parent might say in the other.

Revise and edit your work when you finish. Check all punctuation and spelling. You may have to use a dictionary to help you.

When you are happy with your story, you can make a published copy for your teacher, parent or friend. You could publish it on a computer. What might your mother and father say?

My reasons for not going to school

1 ______________________________

2 ______________________________

3 ______________________________

4 ______________________________

5 ______________________________

____

____

____

____

____

____

____

____

____

Reading for fun

A man rushes into the doctor's surgery. 'I came as soon as I got your message. What's the problem?'

The doctor looks at his notes and says sadly, 'Your lab results have just come back. You only have 24 hours to live.'

'That's terrible!' says the patient.

'There's worse. I've been trying to call you since yesterday!'

Doctor, Doctor! I feel like a strawberry!

Don't worry, I can see you're in a bit of a jam!

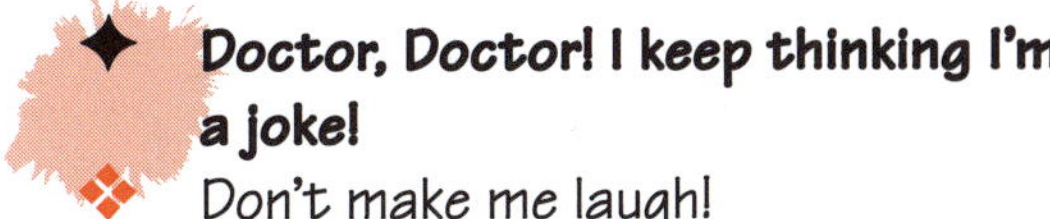

Doctor, Doctor! I keep thinking I'm a joke!

Don't make me laugh!

☞Answers on pages 109–110

Review 1

Now let's see what you remember of the words you learnt in Units 1–5. There are four tests in this review. You could do all in one session, or you could break them up and do them over a few days.

Step 1 Look at each group of words in the test to revise the spellings.

Step 2 Cover the five words up and test yourself (column 2). Try to do all five words in one go.

Step 3 Write your score out of 5 in the box. If you got any words wrong, go back and study them again.

Step 4 If possible, ask someone to test you on the words later—an hour or even a day later (column 3).

Test 1

Study	Test yourself	Test with another person
clothes supermarket nurse dentist parents	/5	/5
dogs leaves path once wizard	/5	/5
ankle hair food bakery butcher	/5	/5
	Total score = out of 15	Total score = out of 15

Test 2

Study	Test yourself	Test with another person
music hairdresser bark musician princess	/5	/5
elf ghost bone hips shopping	/5	/5
banker books plumber policeman barber	/5	/5
chest finger knuckle socks stamps	/5	/5
	Total score = out of 20	Total score = out of 20

Test 3

Study	Test yourself	Test with another person
birds cafe visitors giant ugly	/5	/5
brain nerve health meat shoes	/5	/5
friend teacher builder picnic seats	/5	/5
fireman baker actor playing sport	/5	/5
	Total score = out of 20	Total score = out of 20

Test 4

Study	Test yourself	Test with another person
witch dwarf magic calf heart	/5	/5
fruit chemist doctor driver artist	/5	/5
insects lake troll happily gnome	/5	/5
	Total score = out of 15	Total score = out of 15

Which word?

1. I don't know who ______________ the cake. (*ate, eight*)
2. Mandy ______________ out all the candles on her cake. (*blew, blue*)
3. Did you ______________ the glass when you dropped it? (*brake, break*)
4. I only have $5. I can't ______________ you an ice cream. (*by, buy*)
5. The ______________ was looking for grass under the snow. (*deer, dear*)

☞Answers on page 110

6 On the farm

Quick fun

Name the following objects and animals. The words are from the **Topic spelling list**.

Use this space to write out your topic words the first time. Use your own paper for extra practice.

Rewrite here those you had most trouble with.

Topic spelling list

Use the **LOOK-SAY-COVER-WRITE-CHECK** strategy to learn these words.

farm	feed	planting
market	farmer	wheat
cattle	pigs	fence
harvest	tractor	wool
windmill	scarecrow	shed
sheep	farmhouse	crop

Spelling strategy

Letter patterns: *ar* words

Think of similar words that may help you spell correctly.

Using letter patterns in the middle of words can help you remember how to spell the word. The letters ***ar*** feature in many words, e.g. ***ar*** is the start of the word ***ar****m*.

1 Can you find six words from the **Topic spelling list** with ***ar*** in them? Write them in the box below.

2 How many words do you know that rhyme with *m**ar**k*? Write them in the box below.

Fill in the gaps

Choose words from the **Topic spelling list** to complete the sentences.

1 A person who grows wheat is called a wheat ____________.

2 Water was pumped from the river using a ____________.

3 Name three animals found on farms. ____________ ____________ ____________

4 By the end of the week the wheat was ready to ____________.

5 By six o'clock it was time to ____________ the pigs.

6 When it got dark the farmer went back to the ____________ for a meal.

7 Mum is ____________ poppies in the front garden.

8 Who wants a ride on the little red ____________?

Scarecrows are often seen on farms. Draw a picture of a scarecrow here. Add some birds. Then label your picture.

Tricky words

The words ***flour*** and ***flower*** sound the same but have different spellings. Words that sound the same but have different spellings are called **homophones**.

Word	Meaning	Example
flower	the coloured, sometimes scented, part of a plant that produces seeds	*Jesse's favourite **flower** is the rose.*
flour	made from grinding grain into powder, most often white	***Flour** is used to make bread.*

Roses are **flowers.**

Bread is made from **flour**.

Complete the sentences with the correct word (*flour* or *flower*).

1. The waiter had a red ______________ in her hair.
2. Wattle is the ______________ of Australia.
3. After making cake, Jill had ______________ all over the floor!
4. The baker had to get a bag of ______________ from the pantry.

Looking at … plurals that stay the same

Mostly we add ***s*** to words to make plurals, e.g. *farm* → *farm**s***.

There are some words that are both singular (one) and plural (more than one), e.g. *one sheep* → *a flock of sheep, one fish* → *a school of fish.*

There are some words that end with **s** that we use as both singular and plural, e.g. we say:
*a pair of **trousers*** and *three pairs of **trousers**.*
*one pair of **tweezers*** and *two pairs of **tweezers**.*

Now it's your turn. Can you complete the table? Look at the examples above for help. You could check your answers using a dictionary.

Singular (one)	Plural (more than one)
1 glasses (for reading)	
2 pants	
3 scissors	
4 salmon	
5 starfish	

Proofreading

When Jin-Hie went to her uncle's farm she collected pictures of things she saw and labelled them. She made five spelling mistakes in her labels. Tick the correct words. Put a cross next to each mistake and write the word correctly beside it.

tracter ______________

sheep ______________

windmill ______________

fence ______________

scarcrow ______________

shed ______________

fermer ______________

cattel ______________

pigs ______________

wheet ______________

Vocabulary power

Compound words are two short words joined together to make one longer word, e.g. *basket* + *ball* = *basketball*

Write the two small words that make the words in **bold** below.

1. A place where pigs are kept is called a **pigpen**. ______________ + ______________
2. Land around a farm is called a **farmyard**. ______________ + ______________
3. A leaf from a gum tree is a **gumleaf**. ______________ + ______________
4. Find three compound words from the **Topic spelling list**.

   ______________ ______________ ______________

5. Tick the compound words in the box below.

teaching	gentleman	firewood
window	railway	January
highway	students	storeroom

How many did you find? ☐

Read and learn

Work out the meanings of the words in **bold** by using the context.

The places where animals are kept on farms often have special names. A stable is a **structure** where horses are **groomed** and fed. A pen is a small enclosure for animals such as pigs. Cattle usually roam around a field or paddock. Rabbits can be kept in a hutch. An **enclosed** area where fowl can **wander** and scratch about is called a run, but at night they perch in a roost. Rabbits are **provided** with a hutch and the farm dogs all have kennels.

Circle the answers **a**, **b** or **c** that mean almost the same as the words in **bold** above.

1	structure	a building	b house	c block
2	groomed	a patted	b raced	c brushed
3	enclosed	a unopened	b fenced	c locked
4	wander	a stroll	b stretch	c feed
5	provided	a protected	b supplied	c left

Puzzle

Can you fill in the six missing words from the **Topic spelling list**?

1			F	☐	☐	☐		
2		☐	A	☐	☐	☐	☐	
3	☐	☐	R	☐	☐	☐	☐	
4			M	☐	☐	☐	☐	☐
5		☐	E	☐	☐	☐		
6		☐	R	☐	☐	☐	☐	☐

Clues

1. A place to grow crops.
2. Lots of cows.
3. Bringing in the crop.
4. A place to sell crops.
5. Made of posts and wire.
6. Used to plough fields.

Your turn to write

Imagine you are a farm dog called Boxer. Write about some of the things you do to help on the farm. Write about the following:

- What are some of the dangers of your work?
- How do you have fun?
- Are there any children on the farm you can play with?

At the end of your story, draw a picture of you at work. Revise and edit your work when you finish. Check all punctuation and spelling. You may have to use a dictionary to help you.

When you are happy with your story, you can make a published copy for your teacher, parent or friend. You could publish it on a computer.

Living on a farm

____

____

____

____

____

____

____

____

____

____

Reading for fun

Two farmers were at a sheep sale.

The first farmer said, 'I don't know whether to buy a cow or a bicycle.'

The second farmer replied, 'You'd look very funny riding a cow!'

The first farmer said, 'Not half as funny as I'd look trying to milk a bicycle!'

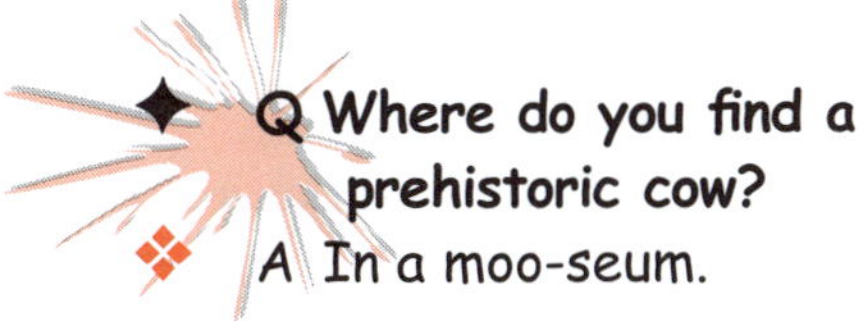

Q Where do you find a prehistoric cow?

A In a moo-seum.

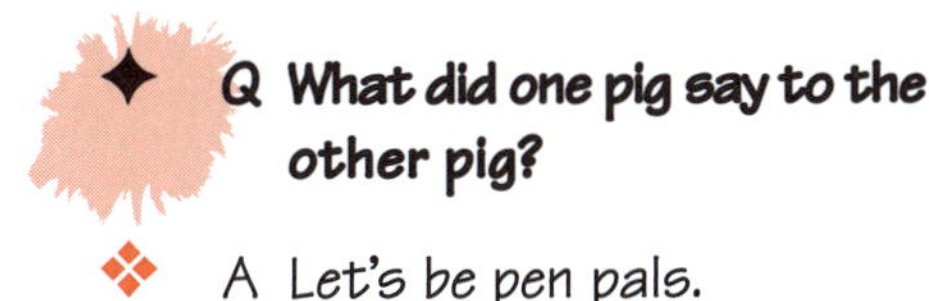

Q What did one pig say to the other pig?

A Let's be pen pals.

Answers on page 110

7 Travelling on

Quick fun

Rewrite the sentences below using spaces. Each sentence has words from the **Topic spelling list**.

1. Didyouarrivebeforethetrain?

____

2. Theguardwasnotatthestation.

____

3. WedepartforourholidayonSunday.

____

4. Wegottothetollroadandhadtopay.

____

Topic spelling list

Use the **LOOK-SAY-COVER-WRITE-CHECK** strategy to learn these words.

highway	ticket	depart
crowd	roads	journey
station	traveller	main
train	guard	arrive
street	toll	tour
travel	holiday	fuel

Use this space to write out your topic words the first time. Use your own paper for extra practice.

____

Rewrite here those you had most trouble with.

____

Spelling strategy

Letter patterns: *ai* words

Think of similar words that may help you spell the word, e.g. *train*:

- Using letter patterns in the middle of words can help you remember how to spell a word.
- The letters ***ai*** are found in many words.
- ***ai*** has the same sound as the letter name for ***a***.
- It rhymes with the letter names for ***k*** and ***j***.

1. Can you find two words from the **Topic spelling list** with ***ai*** in them? Write them in the box below.

2. How many words do you know that rhyme with *m**ai**n* and have ***ai*** in them? Write your words here. The first letter is to start you off.

a	m ____________	**b**	r ____________	**c**	tr ____________	**d**	pl ____________
e	g ____________	**f**	gr ____________	**g**	dr ____________	**h**	p ____________

Fill in the gaps

Choose words from the **Topic spelling list** to complete the gaps in these sentences.

Ms Driver was yelling something about students who (1) ____________________ on buses. I got the message and splashed my way to the bus stop. I was soaked to the skin. Water gushed down drains and across the (2) ____________________ like a wild river. Sticks, leaves, plastic bags and paper swept by as I made a head-down dash for the safety of the buses and the (3) ____________________ back to school.

Somehow I managed to (4) ____________________ onto the bus as the door hissed shut. No need for a (5) ____________________. Waves of (6) ____________________ slammed against the windows. As we started our journey, the windscreen wipers looked as if they were about to snap off as they struggled against the downpour.

Tricky words

The words ***fare*** and ***fair*** sound the same but have different spellings. Words that sound the same but have different spellings are called **homophones**.

Word	Meaning	Example
fare	money paid for a ride	*The bus* ***fare*** *was $2.50.*
fair	1 light in colour	*Eve has* ***fair*** *hair.*
	2 fine weather	*We had* ***fair*** *weather for the picnic.*
	3 according to the rules	*It will be* ***fair*** *if we share the money evenly.*

Complete the sentences with the correct word (*fare* or *fair*).

1. The train ________________ was cheaper than the bus ________________.
2. 'That's not ________________!' called the captain.
3. If the weather is ________________, we can join the crowd at the beach.
4. Who paid the ________________ for my ferry ride?
5. Her skin was ________________ so she avoided sitting in the sun.

Looking at ... unusual plurals

Mostly we add **s** to words to make plurals, e.g. *train* → *train**s***.

Sometimes the singular (one) and plural (more than one) are different words.

We say: *one* ***man*** but *many* ***men***
one ***mouse*** but *many* ***mice***
one ***tooth*** but *many* ***teeth.***

Now it's your turn. Can you complete the table?

Singular (one)	Plural (more than one)
1 goose	
2 foot	
3 child	
4 woman	

Proofreading

Find seven spelling mistakes and write them correctly in the box below.

Then it happened. Just like that. No excuses. A great flash of lightning, a deafening roll of thunder—then the rane. It arived in a flash. Not just steady soaking rain but a deluge. Not buckets. Not cats and dogs. It was as if there was some great waterfall in the sky and we were trapped under it.

My freind, Bobsy, just stared, mouth open, at it until the taecher tapped her under the chin and she slowly closed her moth. She could have drowned in minutes.

Already there was a sheet of water covering the oval. Angry gusts of wind turned it into a choppy laike. A crowed of people were rushing for shelter like drenched rats. I felt like a used tea bag.

Vocabulary power

Sometimes we add ***ist*** to a word to describe the person that does something specific.

A person that treats our **dental** problems is a **dentist**.
A person that goes on a **tour** is a **tourist**.
A person that plays a **harp** is a **harpist**.

What do we call the following people?

1. A person that sings a **solo** is a ______________________.
2. A person that does **art**works is an ______________________.
3. A person that plays an **organ** is an ______________________.
4. A person that writes a **novel** is a ______________________.

Read and learn

Use the context clues to work out the meanings of the words in **bold**.

Didn't sleep much last night. Had bad dreams of swimming *through* the rain because it was so heavy. Couldn't find a surface. Kept getting pounded onto the grass of the athletics oval. I have a very **vivid** idea of what it would be like being flushed down the toilet bowl! I woke up **gasping** for air.

Of course, the news earlier that night didn't help matters. The weatherman came on looking **bewildered**. He tried to explain the extraordinary **deluge** that had hit our carnival during the afternoon. It hadn't been observed on the radar. No **indication** whatsoever. No forecaster saw it. A storm out of the blue he kept saying, shaking his head. No one else in the city had had a similar experience. Just us, and right on the last race. My race! No wonder I had nightmares.

Circle the answers **a**, **b** or **c** that mean almost the same as the words in **bold** above.

1	vivid	**a** clear	**b** bright	**c** clever
2	gasping	**a** panting	**b** holding	**c** gaping
3	bewildered	**a** bored	**b** wild	**c** confused
4	deluge	**a** deluxe	**b** downpour	**c** cyclone
5	indication	**a** sign	**b** warning	**c** message

Puzzle

Fill in this square using the clues and words from the **Topic spelling list**.

1							
2							
3							
4							
5							
6							

Clues

1. You can travel on these from town to town.
2. Get to your destination.
3. You get one when you pay a fare.
4. When you leave.
5. Go from place to place.
6. A person who goes on tours.

Write the letters from the shaded squares here.

1. Now rearrange the letters to make one of the words from the **Topic spelling list**. Write it here. ____________________
2. Write the word from the **Topic spelling list** for the picture above. ____________________

Your turn to write

Pretend you are going on holiday.

Write a five-day diary describing some of the things you did. Remember:

- on day 1 you leave home and arrive at your holiday place.
- on day 5 you leave your holiday place and arrive home.

At the end of your diary, draw a picture of one thing you did during the holiday. Revise and edit your work when you finish.

When you are happy with your diary, you can make a published copy for your teacher, parent or friend. You could publish it on a computer.

Holiday diary

1 ______________________________

2 ______________________________

3 ______________________________

4 ______________________________

5 ______________________________

____

____

____

____

____

____

____

Reading for fun

A lady planned to travel from Sydney to Perth by train. She rang the travel agent and asked how long the trip would take.

'Just a minute,' replied the girl who answered the phone.

'Oh, thank you,' replied the lady and hung up.

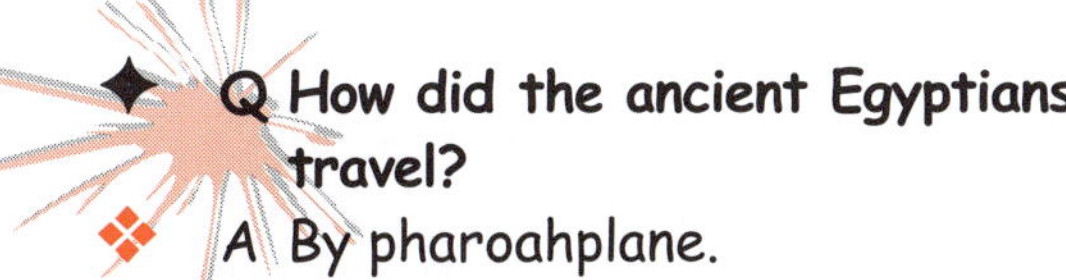

Q How did the ancient Egyptians travel?

A By pharoahplane.

Q What part of a car wants to sleep?

A The wheels. They're always tyred.

☞Answers on page 110

8 Be a sport

Quick fun

Find a word from the **Topic spelling list** for the following pictures.

1 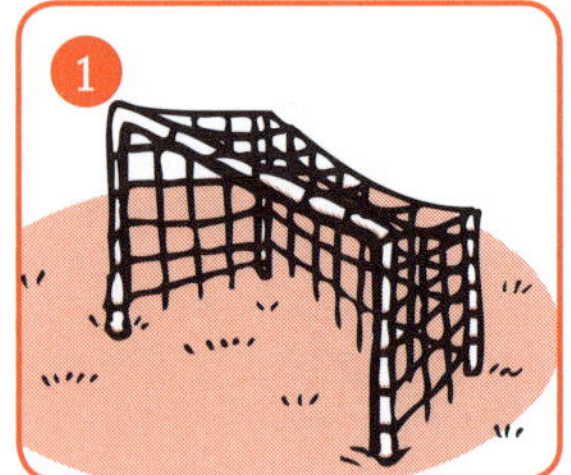

____

2 

____

3 

____

4

____

5 

____

6 This is a circle. This is an ______________________.

Use this space to write out your topic words the first time. Use your own paper for extra practice.

Rewrite here those you had most trouble with.

Topic spelling list

Use the **LOOK-SAY-COVER-WRITE-CHECK** strategy to learn these words.

oval	draw	soccer
cricket	first	winner
goal	starting	swimming
distance	netball	whistle
place	starter	speed
player	cheers	coach

Spelling strategy

The suffix *-ing*

A letter or syllable (group of letters) placed at the end of a word to make a new word is called a **suffix**. Some common suffixes are: ***-s***, ***-es***, ***-ing***, ***-ed***, ***-er***, ***-ness*** and ***-or***.

You have already learned that ***-ist*** can be added to words to describe a person, e.g. a person who wins a **medal** is a **medal***ist*.

Many new words are simply formed by adding the suffix -***ing*** to a word, e.g.
draw → *draw****ing***   *spell* → *spell****ing***   *coach* → *coach****ing***   *start* → *start****ing***

Doing this makes the verb present tense.

There are many words that end with **e**. With these words the **e** is dropped before adding ***ing***, e.g. *mov***e** → *mov****ing***   *writ***e** → *writ****ing***   *plac***e** → *plac****ing***   *driv***e** → *driv****ing***

Now it's your turn to make some ***ing*** words. Can you complete this table with ***ing*** words?

1 mark		2 race	
3 score		4 cheer	
5 play		6 change	
7 fire		8 bowl	
9 form		10 use	

Fill in the gaps

Choose words from the **Topic spelling list** to complete the sentences below.

Sports headlines

The weekend sport gave fans a few shocks. On the sports 1 ______________, a 2 ______________ was warned when he kicked a 3 ______________ ball into the crowd after the final match was declared a two-all 4 ______________.

Mary Brown, who was expected to be a 5 ______________ in the long 6 ______________ race, failed to get a 7 ______________. Her 8 ______________ in the last hundred metres was anything but impressive. Brown will need to train more often.

The 9 ______________posts will be removed from the field next week, and the pitch repaired for the start of the summer 10 ______________ competition. Fast bowler Neville King will lead the local team.

Netball is moving to a new venue out at Newville Park. The 11 ______________ team will 12 ______________ in the Newville Pool Complex next door.

Tricky words

The words ***whole*** and ***hole*** sound the same but have different spellings. Words that sound the same but have different spellings are called **homophones.**

Word	Meaning	Example
whole	complete, including all parts	*Fred ate a* ***whole*** *pie.*
hole	a gap or opening in or through something	*There was a* ***hole*** *in the road.*

Complete the following sentences with the correct word (*whole* or *hole*).

1. Jay lost a ____________________ bag of marbles.
2. 'Who puts the ____________________ in doughnuts?' giggled Loren.
3. The ____________________ school was left waiting for buses!
4. The cigarette burnt a ____________________ in my shirt.
5. Elaine completed the ____________________ jigsaw before the end of the day.

Looking at … *wh* words

Many words start with ***wh***. The ***h*** in these words is usually silent, e.g. ***wh****istle*, ***wh****ere*, ***wh****en*, ***wh****y*, ***wh****ip*, ***wh****ite*, ***wh****arf*, ***wh****ale*, ***wh****at*, ***wh****ole*.

Write the full ***wh*** words on the lines below.

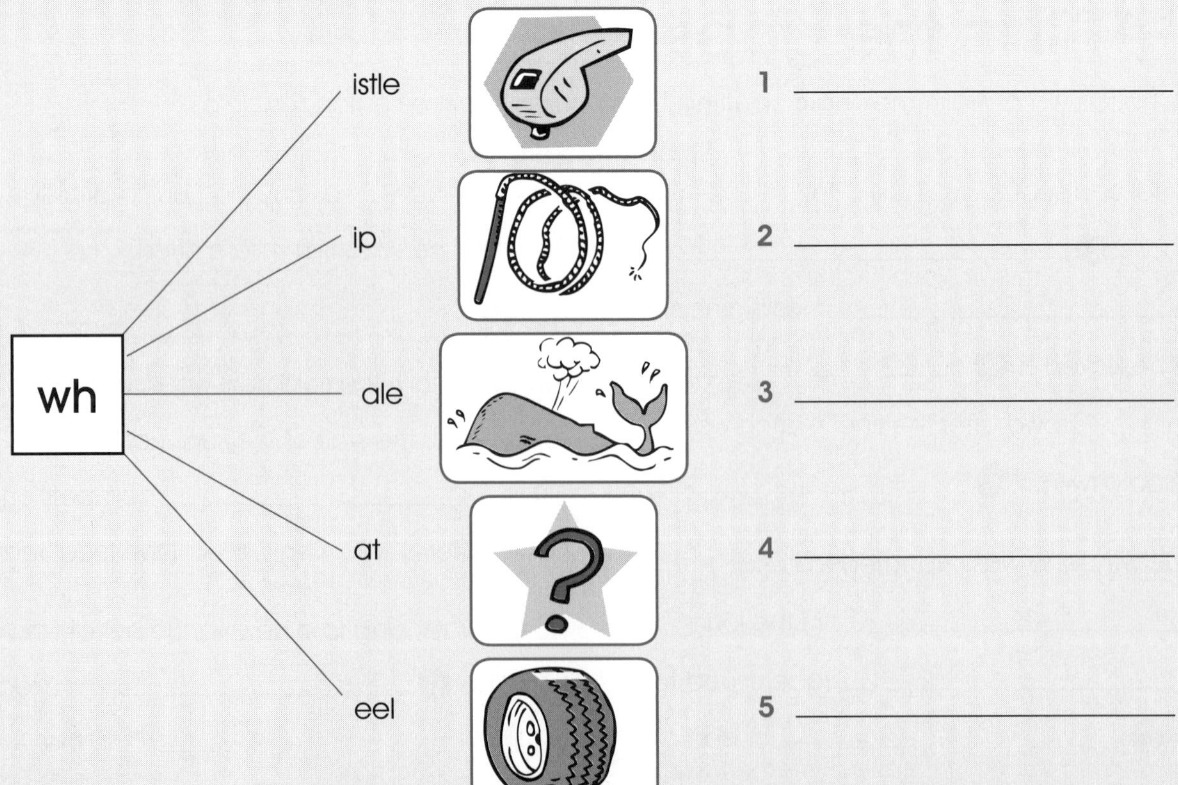

1 ____________________

2 ____________________

3 ____________________

4 ____________________

5 ____________________

Proofreading

Can you find the six spelling mistakes in the text below? Draw a line around the mistakes and write the words correctly in the box below.

People spend their spare time doing many different things. Children are often seen on the ovall playing running games. In our town, young adults trane for sports such as cricket, swimming, soceer, netaball and basketball. Many adults join clubs to play bowls or golf.

My perants don't belong to a club. They prefer to go walking in the parck or just listen to music at home.

Vocabulary power

It's good to know the names of **places where sport can be played**.

Place	Definition	Sport
arena	a large open area surrounded by seating	athletics
stadium	a large covered area surrounded by seats	football, boxing
field	an open area marked for playing games	cricket, football
course	a large open area for sport	running, golf
rink	a level, enclosed area usually of ice	hockey, skating
green	a grassed area, often flat	lawn bowls, golf

Can you name three sporting activities you can do in a pool?

____

____

____

Read and learn

Work out the meanings of the words in **bold**.

The game of soccer officially **appeared** during the late 19th century in England. At this time there were several ball games, all of which **involved** both handling and kicking. At a meeting of a group of people in London in 1863, the game of football was split into rugby, in which handling and carrying the ball was allowed, and association football, which **forbade** the use of the hands.

The Football Association (FA) **established** the first set of soccer rules. At that time, soccer was played competitively only in private schools and universities.

In no time, amateur competition became popular with British workers. The FA Cup, an **annual tournament** first organized in 1871, sparked huge interest in soccer. The tournament, which is still played today, starts with a large pool of teams and finishes with the FA Cup Final at Wembley Stadium in London.

Circle the answers **a**, **b** or **c** that mean almost the same as the words in **bold** above.

		a	b	c
1	appeared	emerged	watched	observed
2	involved	revolved	included	insisted
3	forbade	banned	forecast	finished
4	established	planned	built	created
5	annual	often	exciting	yearly
6	tournament	tour	competition	display

Puzzle

Using the **Topic spelling list**, find words that start with the last letter of each given word below. Write the words from top to bottom in the grid. Here is an example to show you what to do.

R I N K
K N O C K

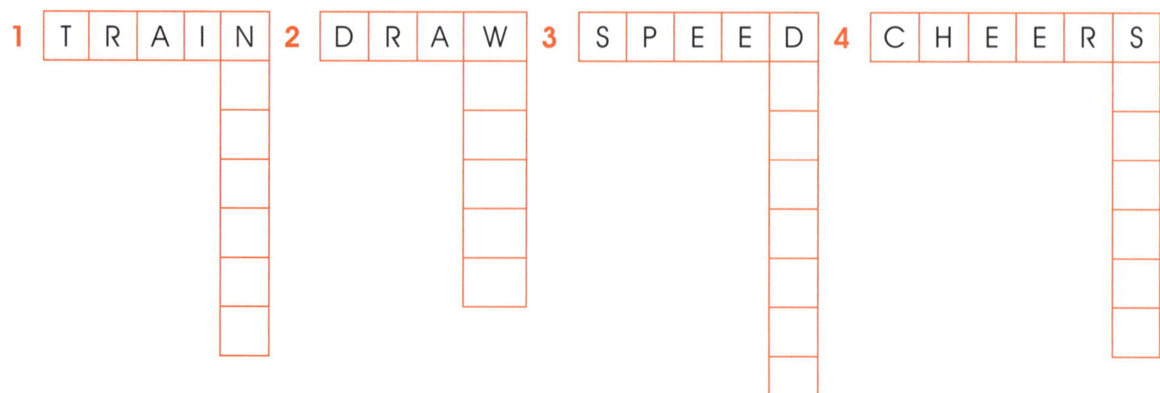

Your turn to write

Your team has just won the Grand Final for ... (you choose the team sport). You are the captain and have to make a speech after receiving the cup.

Write a short speech and thank the people who made your win possible, e.g. the players, the coach, the parents who drove your team to the match each week, the sponsors, etc.

At the end of your writing, draw a picture that looks like a photograph for the local paper. It should show you holding the cup and perhaps shaking hands with the organisers. You could add a caption.

Revise and edit your work when you finish. When you are happy with your speech, you can make a published copy.

Reading for fun

Dan took up skydiving as a sport. On his first solo jump, he pulled the ripcord at the right time, but nothing happened. The parachute wouldn't open. He then pulled the emergency chute, but that didn't open.

As he glanced down to see the ground rushing to him, he saw a man hurtling upward, directly at him.

'Hey!' Dan shouted. 'Do you know anything about parachutes?'

'No!' the man yelled back. 'Do you know anything about gas stoves?'

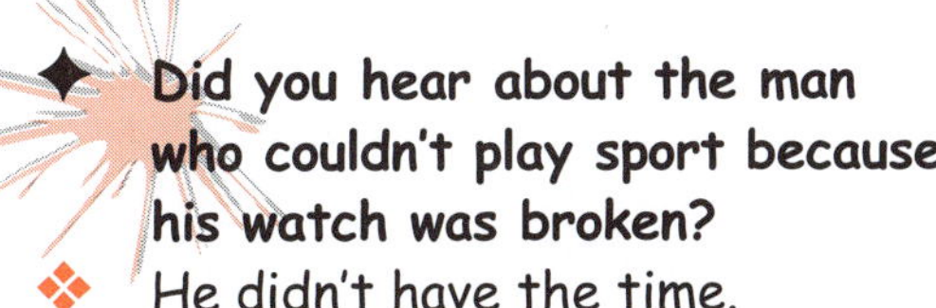

Did you hear about the man who couldn't play sport because his watch was broken?

He didn't have the time.

Did you hear about the karate expert who joined the army?

He knocked himself out when he saluted.

☞Answers on pages 110–111

9 To the zoo

Quick fun

When Ahmed typed some animal names on his computer he left the first letter off by mistake. Can you supply the first letter of these animals? The words are all in the **Topic spelling list**.

1. **a** ☐ion **b** ☐onkey **c** ☐oala **d** ☐anda **e** ☐lephant
   f ☐andicoot **g** ☐iger **h** ☐ear **i** ☐amel **j** ☐ombat

2. What name could you call the following animals?
   lion, tiger, puma, leopard, panther

   They are all big ____________________.

Topic spelling list

Use the **LOOK-SAY-COVER-WRITE-CHECK** strategy to learn these words.

monkey	bandicoot	healthy
crawl	reptile	wombat
elephant	cage	camel
bear	asleep	nesting
visit	tiger	lion
koala	panda	scared

Use this space to write out your topic words the first time. Use your own paper for extra practice.

Rewrite here those you had most trouble with.

Spelling strategy

The suffix *-ed*

You have learned that a letter or syllable (group of letters) placed at the end of a word to make a new word is called a **suffix**.

You have already learned that the suffix -***ing*** can be added to words to make new words, e.g. *visit* ⟶ *visit**ing***, *bite* ⟶ *bit**ing***.

Many new words are simply formed by adding the suffix -***ed*** to a word. This suffix shows things have happened in the past, e.g. *start* ⟶ *start**ed***, *crawl* ⟶ *crawl**ed***, *visit* ⟶ *visit**ed***.

There are many words that end with **e**. For these words we simply add ***d***, e.g. *move* ⟶ *move**d***, *race* ⟶ *race**d***, *hope* ⟶ *hope**d***.

Now it's your turn to make ***ed*** words. Complete the table below.

1 hiss		2 nurse	
3 growl		4 bark	
5 dive		6 act	
7 whistle		8 use	
9 bank		10 glide	

Fill in the gaps

Choose words from the **Topic spelling list** to complete the following sentences.

1. On our last (a) ____________ to the zoo we took our camera. I took a picture of a (b) ____________ with two humps. Mum took a picture of a polar (c) ____________. We saw black snakes and a frill-necked (d) ____________ in the Australian (e) ____________ section. They were all fast (f) ____________ behind glass walls so I wasn't (g) ____________. Dad said the animals looked well-fed and (h) ____________.

2. Name these animals.

____________ ____________ ____________ ____________ ____________

3. Write the names of three Australian animals from the **Topic spelling list**.

____________ ____________ ____________

Tricky words

The words ***bear*** and ***bare*** sound the same but have different spellings. Words that sound the same but have different spellings are called **homophones**.

Word	Meaning	Example
bear	1 a large furry mammal Note: koalas are NOT bears.	*The polar* ***bear*** *lives in snowy country.*
	2 carry a load or suffer pain	*I can't* ***bear*** *the pain!*
bare	1 without covering	*She tripped over and scraped her* ***bare*** *knees.*
	2 empty	*Old Mother Hubbard went to the cupboard but the cupboard was* ***bare****.*

Complete the sentences with the correct word (*bear* or *bare*).

1. A ______________ came out of the forest and stole our food.
2. There were no leaves on the tree. It was ______________.
3. Did the dog ______________ its teeth as you walked past?
4. The office was ______________ after the robbery.
5. Jake walked down the lane in ______________ feet.
6. My brother won't go anywhere without his teddy ______________.

Looking at … alliteration

Sometimes we can make our writing more interesting by using **alliteration**: words that start with the same sound as the word they are next to, e.g. ***g****rowling* ***g****orillas*, ***a****ngry* ***a****nts*, ***b****uzzing* ***b****ees*, ***s****lithering* ***s****nakes*.

1. Can you think of an alliterative adjective for the following words?

   a ______________ wombat **b** ______________ lizard

   c ______________ bear **d** ______________ tortoise

   e ______________ cricket **f** ______________ horse

   Can you add an animal for each of the following adjectives? (You must use alliteration.)

2. **a** toothless ______________ **b** fat ______________ **c** dangerous ______________

Alliteration can be used in the titles of your stories, e.g.

Proofreading

Tamara filled in her calendar for June. She made seven spelling mistakes. Circle the mistakes and write the words correctly next to them.

June						
Sunday	**Monday**	**Tuesday**	**Wednesday**	**Thursday**	**Friday**	**Saturday**
	1 go to netball	2 finish bare cub story	3 change saets with Sue	4 give note to perents	5 cover text book	6
7	8	9	10	11	12 Maths test	13
14	15 return note too school	16	17 school zoo viset	18 hand in homework	19 go shoping	20
21	22 phone Sandy	23	24 Book Club	25	26 by new shoes	27 see Sandy
28	29 go to netball	30 school dance 7 p.m.				

Vocabulary power

There are many different names for **groups of animals**. Look at the table below to find the **collective nouns** for each animal.

Animal	Group	Animal	Group	Animal	Group
bee	swarm	fish	school	seal	pod
dog	pack	sheep	flock	goose	gaggle
elephant	herd	lion	pride	monkey	troop

Use your dictionary to find out what animals form the following groups. (**Note:** there can be more than one correct answer.)

1. plague ______________________
2. colony ______________________
3. brood ______________________
4. cloud ______________________

a mob or troop of kangaroos

a team of bullocks

Read and learn

Use the context clues to work out the meanings of the words in **bold**.

The South Pole (Antarctica) and Australia are the only large land masses that don't have any of the 36 species of the world's wild cat families. Wild cats are spread across most of the globe, excluding these two continents.

The phrase 'big cat' refers to large, wild felines. The term is used to **distinguish** truly large felines, which can weigh over one hundred kilograms, from much smaller wild cat species. **Despite** enormous differences in size, the various species of cat are amazingly similar in both structure and behaviour. All cats are **carnivores** and are very efficient hunters of prey.

The four largest big cats can truly roar, while other cats cannot. The ability to roar is sometimes considered a key **characteristic** of big cats. Cats that cannot roar have vocal chords more **suited** to purring, while roaring cats cannot purr.

Circle the answers **a**, **b** or **c** that mean almost the same as the words in **bold** above.

1. distinguish — **a** watch — **b** tell apart — **c** disturb
2. despite — **a** react — **b** although — **c** but
3. carnivores — **a** cruel — **b** cunning — **c** meat eaters
4. characteristic — **a** feature — **b** marking — **c** shape
5. suited — **a** fitting — **b** dressed — **c** reliable

Puzzle

Can you find the following zoo animals in the wordsearch below?

T	T	I	G	E	R	Y	B	E	A	R	E
H	P	Q	K	O	A	L	A	L	T	Q	I
B	J	V	A	J	P	U	N	E	Z	F	D
L	I	O	N	N	E	E	D	P	F	C	R
L	C	I	G	W	Q	X	I	H	X	A	F
I	P	A	A	L	B	G	C	A	M	M	H
Z	E	B	R	A	K	M	O	N	K	E	Y
A	U	D	O	C	E	R	O	T	G	L	N
R	B	W	O	M	B	A	T	E	M	L	S
D	K	V	D	G	S	T	O	M	D	H	P
C	A	Z	L	W	P	A	N	D	A	Y	O

koala
bandicoot
monkey
camel
bear
wombat
lion
lizard
tiger
kangaroo
elephant
panda
zebra
ape

Your turn to write

In the space below, draw a map of a zoo. Show and label the enclosures (cages). You can add enclosures for animals that are not in the **Topic spelling list**. Show the paths around the zoo. You could put arrows on the paths to show the best way to walk. Remember to make your enclosures different shapes and sizes. They do not have to be square.

You could add a kiosk and a picnic area. A parking area and the main gate are already shown. Draw small pictures of the animals at several of the enclosures.

Revise and edit your work when you finish. Spelling mistakes should be corrected. You may have to use a dictionary to help you.

When you are happy with your map you can show your teacher, parent or friend. You might be able to use a 'Draw' program on your computer to make a published copy.

Zoo Map

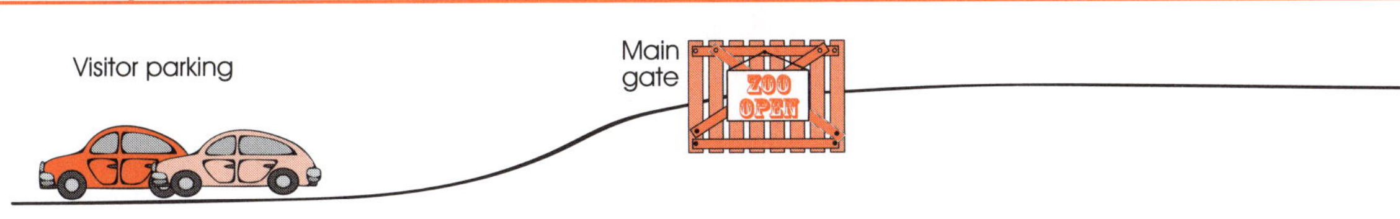

Reading for fun

Zookeeper 1 I've lost one of my elephants.

Zookeeper 2 Why don't you put an advert in the paper?

Zookeeper 3 Don't be silly. My elephant can't read!

Q There are three keys that won't open any door. What are they?

A Donkey, monkey and turkey.

Q What do you get when you cross a dog with an elephant?

A A very nervous postman!

 Answers on page 111

10 Our world

Quick fun

Sometimes we can hide words in sentences.

Look at the sentence below. You will see the word ***shove***. All the letters are in the correct order.

'Da***sh over*** to the store,' said Dad.

Find a word from the **Topic spelling list** in each of these sentences and write it in the boxes.

1. Your back will be aching by tonight.
2. It is a crow or king parrot in the tree.
3. Do trucks tow new cars away?
4. Can Paul count rye seeds on his plate?

Topic spelling list

Use the **LOOK-SAY-COVER-WRITE-CHECK** strategy to learn these words.

city	country	beach
ocean	plain	alps
river	destroy	litter
town	working	explore
earth	planet	mountain
stream	valley	wood

Use this space to write out your topic words the first time. Use your own paper for extra practice.

Rewrite here those you had most trouble with.

Spelling strategy

Letter patterns: *ou* words

When **o** and **u** are side by side in a word, the **o** comes before the **u**. It makes the sound **ow** as in **cow**. Using this trick will help you remember how to spell the word. Look out for other words that follow this pattern.

out	our ouch
round	found ground hound sound mound pound
count	mount mountain fountain

1 Write the two **ou** words from the **Topic spelling list** here.________________

2 How many words do you know that rhyme with *out* and have **ou** in them? Write your words here. The first letters have been done for you.

a AB__________ b B__________ c TR__________

d P__________ e L__________ f ST__________

g SP__________

3 What is the missing word? North, __________, east and west.

Fill in the gaps

Choose words from your **Topic spelling list** to complete the sentences.

1 When he was 16 years old, Dan Walker planned to (a) __________ the stream behind his house. He followed the (b) __________ until it became a small (c) __________ in a narrow (d) __________. The river flowed into a shallow lake. After his walk Jim had a swim. In the distance he could hear the roar of the (e) __________ as waves crashed on the (f) __________. It was then time for the return trip. He headed into a pine (g) __________, then across rocky (h) __________ until he was at the edge of his small (i) __________.

2 High mountains are called ☐☐☐☐.

3 A very large town is called a ☐☐☐☐.

4 An area of trees is called a ☐☐☐☐.

Tricky words

The words ***plain(s)*** and ***plane*** sound the same but have different spellings. Words that sound the same but have different spellings are called **homophones**.

Word	Meaning	Example
plain	1 a large flat area usually with few trees (often ***plains***)	*Wheat is grown on the western* ***plain****.*
	2 simple and undecorated	*John has a* ***plain*** *shirt.*
plane	short word for *aero****plane***	*The band left on a jet* ***plane****.*

Complete the sentences with the correct word (*plain* or *plane*).

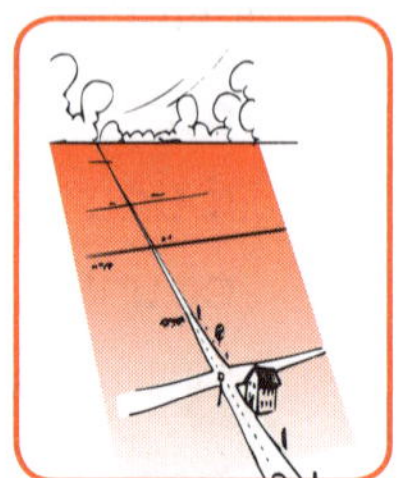

a view of a plain

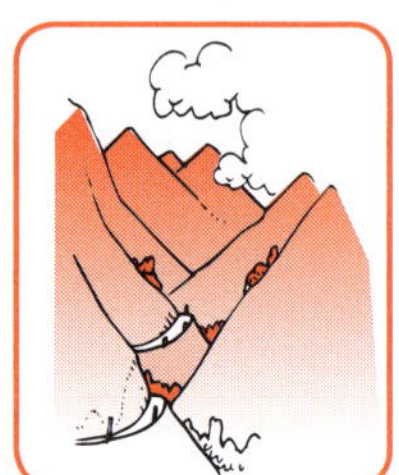

a view of a valley

1. 'After the ________________ landed I looked for my bags,' said the tourist.
2. We watched the ________________ take off.
3. Two plus two equals four. Surely that is ________________ to you!
4. The star has a ________________ face but she is a brilliant actor.
5. There is a mountain and a ________________ to cross before coming to a river.
6. This is an air force fighter ________________.

Looking at ... shortened words

You have learned that ***plane*** is short for ***aeroplane***.

There are many more words that have been **shortened**. Many are now used as the correct word, e.g. the word ***pram*** comes from ***perambulator***! Here are some more examples: ***van*** for *cara****van***, ***pop*** (song) for ***pop****ular*, ***flu*** for *in****flu****enza.*

1. What are the following words short for? You might have to use a dictionary to help you.

   a exam ________________ **b** lab ________________ **c** bus ________________

   d taxi ________________ **e** vet ________________ **f** gym ________________

   Some shortened words are not suitable for all occasions, e.g. *maths*, *crim* and *uni.*

2. What are the short and long words for the following?

a ________________ **b** ________________ **c** ________________

Proofreading

David copied this verse of the poem, 'My Country', by Dorothea Mackellar.

He made seven spelling mistakes. One line has no mistakes.

Circle the mistakes and write the correct spelling opposite. If there are no mistakes in a line, put a tick.

I love a sun-burnt countery, ______________________

A land of sweeping planes, ______________________

Of ragged montain ranges, ______________________

Off droughts and flooding rains. ______________________

I love her far horizons, ______________________

I love her jewel see, ______________________

Her beauty an her terror— ______________________

The wide brown land four me! ______________________

Vocabulary power

We know words can have more than one meaning. Let's look at ***litter***.

Litter can mean:

- rubbish left lying around OR a covering of leaves under trees, e.g. *leaf litter*
- a group of young animals born at the same time, e.g. *a litter of kittens.*

Can you find the words from the **Topic spelling list** that have the following meanings?

1. **a** a large, flat, dry area of land
   b not decorated or marked in any way
   c not pretty, not ugly

   The word is ______________.

2. **a** soil
   b the third planet from the sun
   c dry land; not sea or sky.

   The word is ______________.

3. **a** a narrow, shallow river
   b a large group of people moving in the same direction
   c a flow of liquid or gas

   The word is ______________.

Read and learn

Work out the meanings of the words in **bold** by using the context.

Jamie drifted off into a shallow sleep hoping that he would wake up in **familiar** surroundings.

Morning brought no escape from the nightmare Jamie had stumbled into.

When they set off for the treasure, Jamie was **tethered** to the hobbling Silver but his hands were free. All the men were armed. Some carried digging **implements.** Their first goal was to find a giant tree to the south of Spy Glass Mountain.

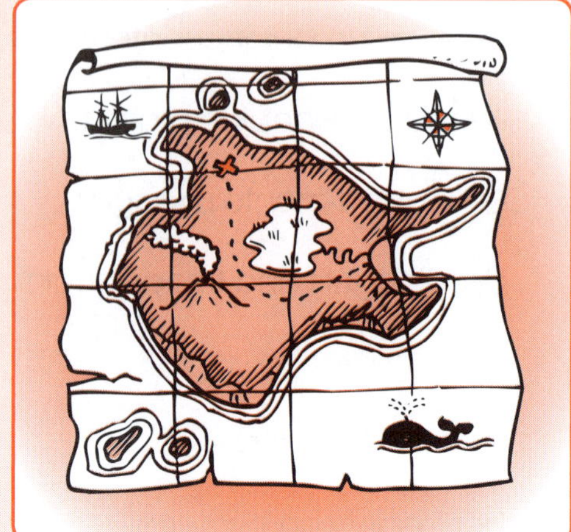

A dispute broke out amongst the pirates as to the map's **interpretation**. Silver warned them to wait until they were closer to the trees in question. They grudgingly agreed that Silver's plan was best.

Suddenly Anderson let out a cry. Everyone stopped.

Circle the answers **a**, **b** or **c** that mean almost the same as the words in **bold** above.

1	familiar	**a** known	**b** common	**c** home
2	tethered	**a** balanced	**b** locked	**c** tied
3	implements	**a** supplies	**b** tools	**c** guns
4	interpretation	**a** lines	**b** location	**c** meaning

Puzzle

Sometimes we can find small words inside big words. The letters are in their correct order. In the word ***beach*** we can find ***be*** and ***each***.

1. How many words can you find in ***mathematics***? Write them in the box below.

2. Now try ***scarecrow***.

Your turn to write

Look back at **Fill in the gaps**.

You are going to do an interview with Dan Walker and ask him about the exploring he did. Your interview will be recorded in the school newsletter.

The interview has been started for you. You will be the **interviewer**. At the end of your interview, draw a picture of Dan on his journey. Add a caption. Revise and edit your work when you finish. Check all punctuation and spelling. You may have to use a dictionary to help you.

When you are happy with your interview, you can make a published copy for your teacher, parent or friend. You could publish it on a computer.

Interview with Dan Walker

Interviewer Good morning, Dan. I'd like to ask you a few questions about the time you explored the stream.

Dan That's fine.

Interviewer Where did you start exploring?

Dan I started in the small stream behind our house.

Interviewer ____

____

____

____

____

____

____

____

____

____

Reading for fun

The teacher called on Yoli to go to the map and point out where the Blue Mountains were.

Yoli looked at the map, found the Blue Mountains, and proudly said, 'Here they are, right here!'

'Very good, Yoli,' the teacher said. 'Now, who can tell me who discovered the Blue Mountains?'

In a flash, Wilbur called out, 'Yoli did, Sir!'

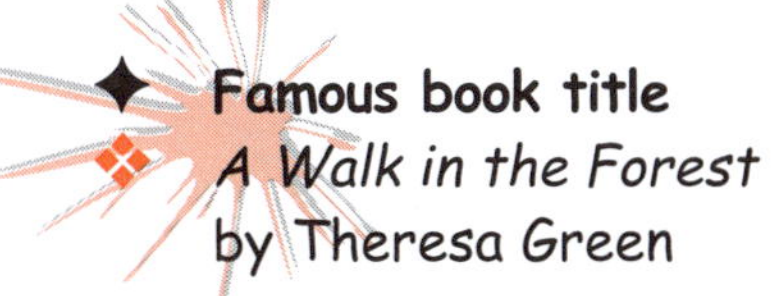

Famous book title
A Walk in the Forest
by Theresa Green

Q What do you get when you cross the Atlantic Ocean wih the Titanic?
A Half way!

Review 2

Now let's see what you remember of the words you learnt in Units 5–10. There are four tests in this review. You could do all in one session, or you could break them up and do them over a few days.

Step 1 Look at each group of words in the test to revise the spellings.

Step 2 Cover the five words up and test yourself (column 2). Try to do all five words in one go.

Step 3 Write your score out of 5 in the box. If you got any words wrong, go back and study them again.

Step 4 If possible, ask someone to test you on the words later—an hour or even a day later (column 3).

Test 1

Study	Test yourself	Test with another person
farmer market cattle highway crowd	/5	/5
station oval cricket goal monkey	/5	/5
crawl elephant city ocean river	/5	/5
	Total score = out of 15	Total score = out of 15

Test 2

Study	Test yourself	Test with another person
harvest windmill sheep street travel	/5	/5
train place visit koala town	/5	/5
earth stream feed roads tickets	/5	/5
little planting wool shed fuel	/5	/5
	Total score = out of 20	Total score = out of 20

Test 3

Study	Test yourself	Test with another person
player first starting reptile cage	/5	/5
country destroy tractor scarecrow holiday	/5	/5
netball starter cheers asleep tiger	/5	/5
arrive whistle speed train nesting	/5	/5
	Total score = out of 20	Total score = out of 20

Test 4

Study	Test yourself	Test with another person
panda working planet guard wheat	/5	/5
fence journey main depart soccer	/5	/5
winner swimming wombat camel beach	/5	/5
	Total score = out of 15	Total score = out of 15

Which word?

1. The baker used plain ____________ in the cake. (*flower, flour*)
2. The ____________ on the ferry was $5.00. (*fare, fair*)
3. Did you see the ____________ in the road? (*hole, whole*)
4. I don't have a hat. My head is ____________. (*bare, bear*)
5. The river cuts across the ____________ to the sea. (*plain, plane*)

☞Answers on page 112

11 What's your number?

Quick fun

Can you fill in the missing words in this old counting rhyme?

One, ______________, ______________, ______________, five

Once I caught a fish alive.

Six, ______________, ______________, nine, ten,

Then I let it go again!

Why did I let it go?

Because it bit my finger so.

Which finger did it bite?

This little finger on the ______________.

Topic spelling list

Use the **LOOK-SAY-COVER-WRITE-CHECK** strategy to learn these words.

three	twenty	dozen
four	thirty	total
seven	forty	estimate
eight	fifty	century
eleven	hundred	numeral
twelve	fourteen	number

Use this space to write out your topic words the first time. Use your own paper for extra practice.

Rewrite here those you had most trouble with.

Spelling strategy

Letter patterns: words starting with *tw*

Words that start with ***tw*** are quite common, e.g. ***tw****ist*, ***tw****ig*, ***tw****it*, ***tw****ist*, ***tw****ine*.

1 Write the numbers that go with these ***tw*** words.

a two ______________

b twelve ______________

c twin ______________

d twenty ______________

e twice ______________

2 Now write the words that go with these numbers.

a 8 ______________

b 40 ______________

c 14 ______________

d 12 ______________

e 24 ______________

Remember
The word ***forty*** (40) is a tricky word. It does NOT have a ***u*** in it like the word ***four*** (4)!

Fill in the gaps

Choose words from the **Topic spelling list** to complete this old nursery rhyme.

The rhyme has some old-fashioned words. This is what they mean:
delve = dig, a'courting = dating, a'waiting = serving, platter = plate.

One, ______________, buckle my shoe.

______________, ______________, knock at the door.

Five, six, pick up sticks.

______________, ______________, lay them straight.

Nine, ten, a big fat hen.

______________, ______________, dig and delve.

Thirteen, ______________, maids a'courting.

Fifteen, sixteen, maids in the kitchen.

Seventeen, eighteen, maids a'waiting.

Nineteen, ______________, my platter's empty.

Tricky words

The words ***four*** and ***for*** sound the same but have different spellings. Words that sound the same but have different spellings are called **homophones**.

The word ***forty*** is another **tricky word**.

Word	Meaning	Example
four	a number: 4	***Four*** *birds sat on a wire.*
for	1 showing place or time 2 wanting a reason	*I'll be there in time* ***for*** *meals.* *What did you come* ***for****?*
forty	a number: 40 (NOT fo**u**rty)	*Ali Baba and the* ***forty*** *thieves.*

Complete the sentences with the correct word (*four, for* or *forty*).

1. Ten, twenty, thirty, ______________________, fifty.
2. Two, ______________________, six, eight, Mary at the cottage gate.
3. What did you come ______________________?
4. I will use that paint ______________________ the front door.
5. ______________________ and twenty blackbirds were baked in a pie!
6. Write the following numbers in words.
   a 44 ______________ **b** 4 ______________ **c** 40 ______________ **d** 14 ______________

Proofreading

Circle the six mistakes in the counting rhyme and write the words correctly in the box below.

Turtles

One turtle baby alone and new,
Finds a freind, and then there are too.
Two baby turtles crawl down to the see,
They find another, and then there are three.
Three baby turtles crawl along the shore,
They find another, and then there are for.
For baby turtles go four a dive,
Up swims another, and then there are five.

Looking at … plurals: words ending in *y*

Some words change from one item to more than one by adding ***es***.
You add ***s*** to words that end in a vowel + ***y***.

one t**oy**	two toy**s**
one monk**ey**	two monkey**s**
one tr**ay**	two tray**s**

If the word ends with a consonant before the ***y***, we must change the ***y*** to ***i*** before adding ***es.***

one ba**by**	two bab**ies**
one po**ny**	two pon**ies**
one f**ly**	two fl**ies**

1 Now try these.

a one bay	two	**b** one day	two
c one lady	two	**d** one berry	two
e one worry	many	**f** one city	two

2 **a** While playing cricket, Dan hit a century but Terry hit two ____________________.

b I know two twos are four and two ____________________ are forty.

Vocabulary power

Sometimes people say things that make little sense, but we know exactly what they are talking about. These sayings are called **idioms**, e.g. when someone says they are going to 'hit the road' they actually mean they are about to leave.

Can you draw a line from the following idioms that use numbers to their meanings?

number one	myself, me
on cloud nine	a short sleep
put two and two together	dressed very nicely
two's company, three's a crowd	it's the same thing
forty winks	very happy
dressed to the nines	two people together are okay, but three people together cause problems
the one and only	something special; there is only one of something
six of one and half a dozen of the other	work something out

Read and learn

Use the context clues to work out the meanings of the words in **bold**.

Playing Cricket

A **match** is played on a field between two sides, each with a total of eleven players, one being the captain. However, by agreement a match may be played between sides of more or less than eleven players. No more than eleven players may field at any one **instance**.

Two sets of wickets, each with three wooden stumps, are **situated** at opposite ends of the pitch. Each set of stumps has two wooden bails on top. A bowler tries to hit the wicket with the cricket ball while the batsman **protects** the wicket.

Scores are called runs. A run is scored when the batsmen run 'safely' from end to end. Runs are also given when a batsman hits the ball along the ground to the boundary for a 'four' or over the boundary without bouncing for a 'six'.

Circle the answers **a**, **b** or **c** that mean almost the same as the words in **bold** above.

1	match	a competition	b sticks	c similar
2	instance	a position	b minute	c time
3	situated	a nearby	b placed	c selected
4	protects	a hides	b guards	c covers

Puzzle

Make your own wordsearch. How many numbers (in words) can you fit into the grid below? Your words should only run from left to right or top to bottom. You can also use numbers that are not in the **Topic spelling list**. Write your number words on the lines at the sides of the grid.

How many words did you use? ____________

Your turn to write

You have just won a long distance race or maybe a fun run.

Describe your race. Talk about the start, what happened along the way, who your main opponents were, how you felt at various stages (kilometres) throughout the race, what the spectators were like, how it felt to break the finishing tape, etc. At the end of your story, draw a picture of that moment.

Revise and edit your work when you finish. Check all punctuation and spelling. You may have to use a dictionary.

When you are happy with your story, you can make a published copy.

Reading for fun

A policeman pulled over a driver for speeding.

'Do you realise that you were driving one hundred kilometres per hour in a fifty zone?' asked the policeman.

'That can't be right,' said the driver. 'I've only been in the car for twelve minutes!'

Teacher: If I had six oranges in one hand and seven in the other, what would I have?

Kate: Big hands, Sir!

Teacher: What do you get when you add twenty-four, fifty and forty-eight, and then subtract fourteen?

Sammy: The wrong answer!

Answers on page 112

12 Water, water

Quick fun

Can you unscramble these words from the **Topic spelling list**?

1 ROLIAS		2 TRAWEY	
3 PACTANI		4 SEUGBREM	
5 FRSTYEEEL		6 OCEAN	
7 ORWRE		8 TREKAN	
9 FRACUSE		10 GHOURDT	

11 Name the passenger ship that hit an iceberg and sank on its first trip?

____

Topic spelling list

Use the **LOOK-SAY-COVER-WRITE-CHECK** strategy to learn these words.

waterless	downpour	kayak
watery	tanker	float
submarine	rower	captain
drought	canoe	skiing
ferry	surface	marine
freestyle	submerge	sailor

Use this space to write out your topic words the first time. Use your own paper for extra practice.

Rewrite here those you had most trouble with.

Spelling strategy

The *-y* suffix

The ***y*** on the end of many words means 'full of' or 'has a lot of'. If your room is *mess**y***, it is full of mess. If the soup is *water**y***, it contains a lot of water. These words are usually adjectives (describing words).

Which word ending in ***y*** means …

1. covered in dirt? ____________
2. covered in grass? ____________
3. has lots of sand? ____________
4. looks a bit like milk? ____________
5. covered in thorns? ____________
6. covered in snow? ____________
7. a lot of wind? ____________
8. covered in frost? ____________
9. Which ***y*** word, from the words above, would be a good name for this snowman?

F____________

Fill in the gaps

1. Choose words from the **Topic spelling list** to match the following definitions.

a a very dry season ____________ **b** the person in charge ____________

c an undersea vessel ____________ **d** someone who rows ____________

e a swimming stroke ____________ **f** rhymes with *merry* ____________

g a ship to carry oil ____________ **h** without water ____________

2. Choose the correct captions for the following pictures.

a

b

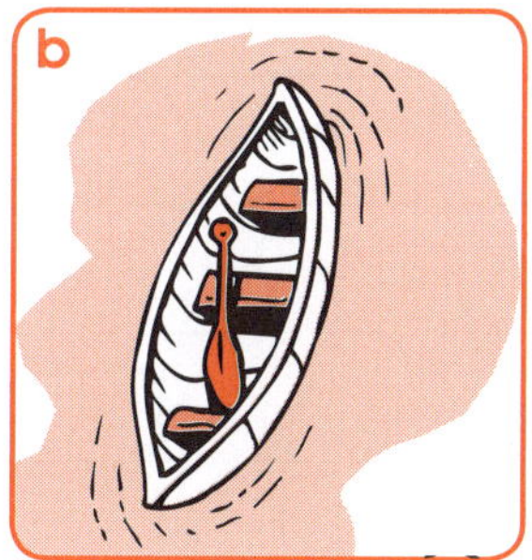

c

d

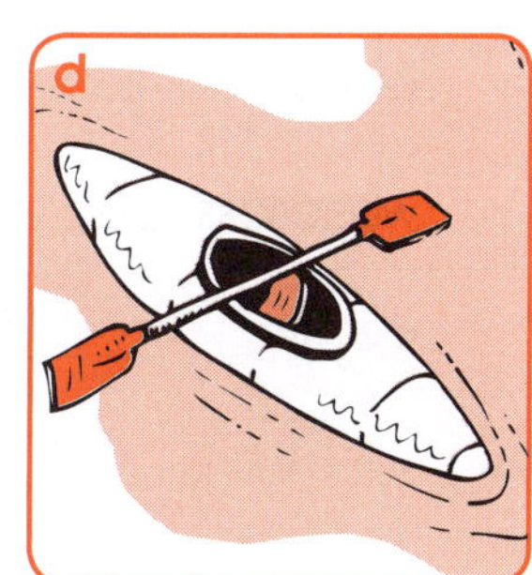

____________ ____________ ____________ ____________

Tricky words

The words ***ferry*** and ***fairy*** sound the same but have different spellings. Words that sound the same but have different spellings are called **homophones**.

Word	Meaning	Example
ferry	a passenger ship	*Ms Bellini took the **ferry** to work each day.*
fairy	a very small winged creature with human shape	*The tooth **fairy** left $1 for my sister's tooth.*

Here is a ferry.

Here is a fairy.

Here are two fairies.

Complete the sentences with the correct word (*ferry* or *fairy*).

1. The ______________________ leaves at eight o'clock to cross the harbour.
2. A ______________________ called Tinker Bell is in the book, *Peter Pan and Wendy*.
3. There is a ______________________ for cars to cross the river.
4. Cinderella had a ______________________ godmother.
5. My parents took a ______________________ trip down the River Nile.

Proofreading

Marty was given a spelling test at home. Mark his work with ticks and crosses. Write any mistakes correctly on the lines between the columns.

sailer	________________	drought	________________	downpoor	________________
canoe	________________	kayak	________________	sking	________________
warterless	________________	ferry	________________	tanker	________________
rower	________________	float	________________	merine	________________
submarine	________________	freestyle	________________	serface	________________
submerg	________________	captain	________________	watery	________________

How many mistakes did Marty make? ________________

Looking at … palindromes

Some words can be read forwards and backwards without changing the word.
These words are called **palindromes**, e.g. ***kayak*** is a palindrome.
Some people's names are palindromes, e.g. Bob, Hannah, Elle, Eve.

1. What part of the face is a palindrome? (**Clue**: it has three letters.) ____________

2. What palindromes am I thinking of below? (The number of letters are shown.)

   a MIDDAY: N ___ ___ ___

   b FLAT: L ___ V ___ ___

   c FEMALE SHEEP: ___ W ___

   d MOTHER: M ___ ___

3. Can you add three-letter palindromes to the table below? The first line has been done for you. If you can't find a word, put a cross.

First and last letter	Middle letter				
	a	*e*	*i*	*o*	*u*
b	X	X	bib	bob	bub
d					
p					
g					
w					

Did you know?

There are very few common words with ***ii***. Three examples are *ski**i**ng*, *taxi**i**ng* (the movement of an aeroplane on the ground) and *Hawa**ii***.

Vocabulary power

For some words, adding ***sub*** to the start (a **prefix**) makes a word that means 'under' or 'getting below', e.g. ***sub**marine* means 'under the marine (sea)', ***sub**total* means 'under the total of an amount before the final total'.

Using the prefix ***sub-***, write the words that match the following definitions.

1. A **way** under the ground is a ____________.
2. A **title** under the main title is a ____________.
3. **Soil** under the top layer of soil is ____________.
4. A speed less than **sonic** is ____________ (a speed **over** sonic is ***super**sonic*!).
5. A person or animal who is less than **human** is ____________.

Read and learn

Work out the meanings of the words in **bold** by using the context.

Newsflash: Oil Spill

Strong winds and rough seas are **hampering** efforts to **tackle** the disaster off Spain after a tanker **laden** with sticky oil broke up and sank.

The giant oil spill from the tanker has led to calls for better controls on the movement of single-hulled oil tankers in coastal waters.

An **armada** of clean-up vessels from around Europe has approached the scene but huge waves have prevented them containing oil on the surface.

Winds are threatening to blow oil ashore from the tanker, which **fractured** during a storm last Wednesday.

Ecologists and volunteers are racing to rescue tar-coated sea birds and clear the black sludge covering more than 80 km of coastline.

Circle the answers **a**, **b** or **c** that mean almost the same as the words in **bold** above.

1	hampering	**a** hindering	**b** fixing	**c** helping
2	tackle	**a** bring down	**b** deal with	**c** rescue
3	laden	**a** lead	**b** fitted	**c** loaded
4	armada	**a** fleet	**b** battle	**c** emergency
5	fractured	**a** sank	**b** bent	**c** cracked

Puzzle

This is the key to solving words in code.

A	B	C	D	E	F	G	H	I	J	K	L	M
1	2	3	4	5	6	7	8	9	10	11	12	13

N	O	P	Q	R	S	T	U	V	W	X	Y	Z
14	15	16	17	18	19	20	21	22	23	24	25	26

1. What are these coded words from the **Topic spelling list**?

   a 6, 5, 18, 18, 25 ______________ **b** 3, 1, 16, 20, 1, 9, 14 ______________

   c 4, 18, 15, 21, 7, 8, 20 ______________ **d** 11, 1, 25, 1, 11 ______________

   e 23, 1, 20, 5, 18, 25 ______________ **f** 19, 11, 9, 9, 14, 7 ______________

   g 18, 15, 23, 5, 18 ______________ **h** 13, 1, 18, 9, 14, 5 ______________

2. Write the following words using the code.

   a submarine ______________ **b** downpour ______________

Your turn to write

Use your dictionary to find a definition for each boat below. Write the definitions in the boxes and then add one fact about each type of boat. Then draw a picture of each boat.

When you are happy with your description, you can make a published copy.

canoe

tanker

ferry

kayak

Reading for fun 1

Knock, knock.
Who's there?
Canoe.
Canoe who?
Canoe come over and help me?

Reading for fun 2

Knock, knock.
Who's there?
Water.
Water who?
Water you doing in my house?

Q What did the Pacific Ocean say to the Atlantic Ocean?

A Nothing. It just waved.

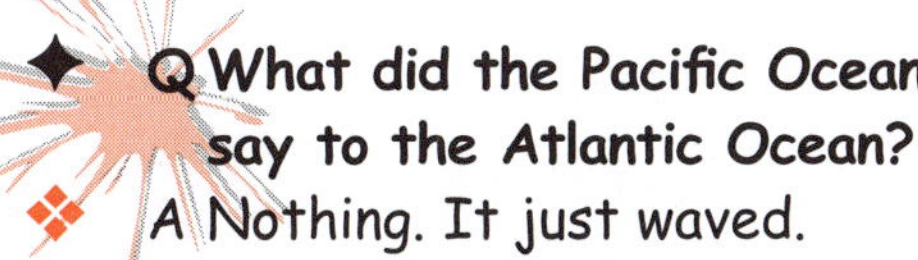

Q What do you call a ferry that lies on the bottom of the ocean and shakes?

A A nervous wreck!

Answers on page 112

13 What did you say?

Quick fun

Circle the word that is least like the others. Then write it on the line. It will be a word from the **Topic spelling list**.

1. yell, whisper, shout, scream, roar

   ____

2. ask, question, reply, enquire, quiz

   ____

3. argue, discuss, quarrel, disagree, row

   ____

4. giggle, growl, moan, sigh, argue

   ____

5. quiet, silent, hushed, speechless, laugh

   ____

Topic spelling list

Use the **LOOK-SAY-COVER-WRITE-CHECK** strategy to learn these words.

answer	reply	discussion
whisper	speechless	think
softly	language	laugh
argue	discuss	silent
sigh	question	thought
tongue	slang	giggle

Use this space to write out your topic words the first time. Use your own paper for extra practice.

Rewrite here those you had most trouble with.

Spelling strategy

Letter patterns: *igh* words

The letters ***igh*** rhyme with the letter name of ***i***. The word *s**igh*** rhymes with *h**igh*** and *by*. A *sigh* is a soft breathing out sound.

Many ***igh*** words end with ***ight***, e.g. *l**ight***, *r**ight*** and *n**ight***.

This is a **light**.

Complete the sentences with ***igh*** or ***ight*** words.

1. When you march you go left, ________________, left ________________.
2. Jan got the problem wrong, but Zoe got it ____________________.
3. I can't walk any more. My shoes are too ______________________.
4. How _______________________ is that hill?
5. Jamie let out a _______________________ when he lost his homework.

This is **sunlight**.

Fill in the gaps

Choose words from the **Topic spelling list** to complete the following sentences.

1. The soft laugh of a child is often called a _______________________.
2. When we talk softly, we talk in a _______________________.
3. If you are asked a ____________________ politely, you should give an ____________________.
4. After the car accident, the _______________________ quickly turned into an argument.
5. Jack _______________________ he could spell *roar*, but he got it wrong.
6. The _______________________ of many Australians is English.
7. To speak, we need to use our vocal cords, lips and _______________________.
8. In class we speak correctly, but it's okay to use _______________________ in the playground.

Tricky words

The words ***roar*** and ***raw*** sound the same but have different spellings. Words that sound the same but have different spellings are called **homophones**.

Word	Meaning	Example
roar	loud growling noise	*The lion gave a **roar**.*
raw	1 not cooked	*I like **raw** carrots but I don't eat **raw** meat!*
	2 uncovered, painful cut or wound	*My face was **raw** from the sun.*

1. Complete the blanks with the correct word (*roar* or *raw*).

   a They say ______________ fruit is good for your teeth.

   b 'Why did the coach ______________ at the team?' questioned the parents.

   c Somewhere in the zoo we heard the ______________ of a wild animal.

   d Pam's heel was rubbed red ______________ because her shoe was too tight.

2. Put a tick in the boxes next to the animals that roar.

tiger ☐ elephant ☐ dog ☐ lion ☐

Looking at … adverbs with *ly*

We can add ***ly*** to many words. Words with the ***-ly*** suffix show **how** or **when** things are done, e.g. *Mary spoke soft**ly***. Many ***ly*** words are called **adverbs** because they describe verbs. Adverbs can make your writing more interesting.

1. Circle the ***ly*** adverbs in the paragraph below.

   Slowly and quietly Emma crossed the room. Her father was sleeping soundly on the couch. Carefully she picked up the purring cat and carried it gently to the kitchen. The cat's saucer was completely empty.

2. Choose the best adverbs from the list to complete the paragraph below.

   sadly hopefully quickly lonely happily fairly neatly slowly

Jason looked (a) ______________ at his messy room. His mother would be home soon. He'd have to work (b) ______________ to clean it up. He picked up his books and placed them (c) ______________ on his desk. He pushed his shoes under the bed. (d) ______________ his mother wouldn't see them. Ever so (e) ______________ he made his bed.

Proofreading

Neera copied this poem from a poetry book. She made six mistakes. Circle the mistakes and write the words correctly in the box below.

The Wind

The wind was angry yesterday,
It howled and rawed around,
Like some huge gaint, sobbing
As it strode across the ground.
Mixed with the wind was flooding rain
That fell like giant tears,
And groans like giant's creaking bones
Filled all the land with fears.

It ripped the branchs from the trees
And tossed them on the ground,
The poor bruised flours dropped their heads,
The leaves fell burnt and browned.
And wen the land was bruised and torn
And darkness turned to day,
It turned its back upon the land
And quietly sliped away.

Elaine Horsfield

Vocabulary power

Many words have the suffix ***-less***. It means 'without'. Here are some examples:

*water**less*** means 'without water', e.g. *the desert was **waterless***.

*speech**less*** means 'without speech', e.g. *I was **speechless** when I won first prize*.

Which ***less*** words could you use instead of the words in **bold** below.

1. There was no **point** in fixing the camera. It was ____________________.
2. Neither team was able to **score** a goal. It was a ____________________ draw.
3. Jenny had no **fear** in the bush. Jenny was ____________________.
4. After winter there was no **colour** in the garden. It was ____________________.
5. The cup is of no **use** after breaking the handle. The cup is ____________________.
6. This man is not wearing a **hat**. He is ____________________.

Read and learn

Use the context clues to work out the meanings of the words in **bold**.

I sighed. Then I sighed again.

'Krystal Creek, stop sighing and find something to do!' growled my father.

'Can't do anything. It's snowing,' I sighed.

Dad looked up from his newspaper. He **puckered** his lips.

Maybe I'd been sighing too much, but I was bored. I waited for Dad's **response**.

'Why don't you ...' He was searching for ideas. '... build a snowman?'

I raised my eyebrows. I shouldn't have!

'Well, if that's too much trouble, I'll tell you what!' he smiled **meanly**. Here it comes, I thought. One sigh too many, for sure! 'If you can find two snowflakes with the same pattern, I'll give you five dollars.' That got a **suspicious** look.

'I'll make it ten!' he **proposed**.

Circle the answers **a**, **b** or **c** that mean almost the same as the words in **bold** above.

1 puckered	a	licked	b	pursed	c	wiped
2 response	a	reason	b	reaction	c	offer
3 meanly	a	quickly	b	widely	c	unkindly
4 suspicious	a	doubtful	b	sudden	c	dishonest
5 proposed	a	promised	b	planned	c	suggested

Puzzle

Here's a chance to use your word knowledge! Can you think of a different *say/said* word starting with every letter of the alphabet? There are some in the **Topic spelling list**. Try to get at least 12.

a		b		c	
d		e		f	
g		h		i	
j		k		l	
m		n		o	
p		q		r	
s		t		u	
v		w		x	
y		z			

Your turn to write

Write an imaginary conversation between you and a friend about something that is important to you, e.g. school, sport, homework, etc. You don't have to agree. Try not to use *said* too often. Try to use the variety of *said* words in this unit. Put inverted commas (' ') around the words spoken.

At the end of your story, draw a picture of you and your friend. Put part of your conversation in the speech bubbles.

Revise and edit your work when you finish. Check all punctuation and spelling. You may have to use a dictionary to help you.

When you are happy with your conversation, you can make a published copy.

A conversation

Note: every time there is a change in speakers, start a new line (paragraph).

____

____

____

____

____

____

____

____

____

____

____

____

Reading for fun

Mr and Mrs Dimwhistle were going on their first overseas holiday. Mrs Dimwhistle had spent a lot of time worrying about what she should take with her. At last they arrived at the airport with all their bags.

'We can start to relax,' whispered Mr Dimwhistle as they waited in line.

'I wish I'd brought the television,' sighed Mrs Dimwhistle.

'Whatever for?' asked Mr Dimwhistle, looking at all their luggage.

'I left the tickets on it,' replied his wife.

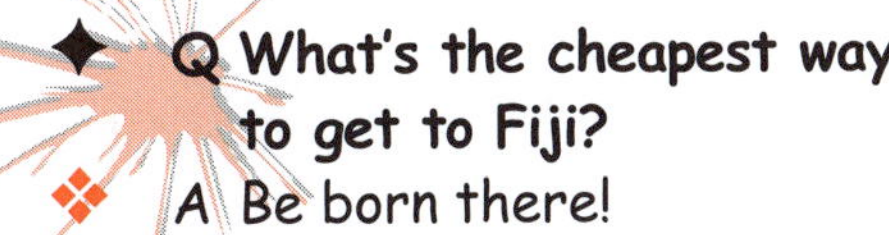

Q What's the cheapest way to get to Fiji?

A Be born there!

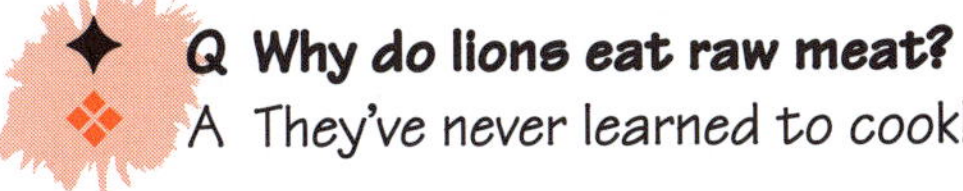

Q Why do lions eat raw meat?

A They've never learned to cook!

☞Answers on page 113

14 For the birds

Quick fun

Sometimes we can hide words in sentences. Look at the sentence below. You will see the word ***grown*** in the sentence. All the letters are in the correct order.

*There was a bi**g row n**ear the office.*

Find a word from the **Topic spelling list** in each of these sentences and write them in the boxes.

1. Deer are eaten by lions.
2. 'A proper chain won't break!' called Dad.
3. The feat her sister performed was amazing.
4. Can we bring in groups of twelve?
5. Switch off lights when you leave the room!

Topic spelling list

Use the **LOOK-SAY-COVER-WRITE-CHECK** strategy to learn these words.

magpie	feathers	parrot
wren	nectar	forest
rare	beak	ringing
flight	eagle	prey
galah	honeyeater	common
perch	brightly	warble

Use this space to write out your topic words the first time. Use your own paper for extra practice.

Rewrite here those you had most trouble with.

Spelling strategy

Letter patterns: words ending in *ar*, *er* and *or*

Words that end with ***ar***, ***er*** and ***or*** often have endings that sound much the same. This can be confusing. Often you will recognise the correct spelling if you write the word down. It is important to learn these endings. Use a dictionary when in doubt. Here are some examples:

~~tractar~~, ~~tracter~~, tractor	The ***or*** ending is correct.
dollar, ~~doller~~, ~~dollor~~	The ***ar*** ending is correct.

Can you select the correctly spelled words below? Draw a line through the mistakes.

1. nectar, necter, nector
2. fathar, father, fathor
3. soccar, soccer, soccor
4. actar, acter, actor
5. motar, moter, motor
6. solar, soler, solor
7. sugar, suger, sugor
8. visitar, visiter, visitor

Fill in the gaps

Choose words from the **Topic spelling list** to complete the following sentences.

The Wedge-tailed Eagle is found across Australia, from sea level to high mountains. It is the most common of the world's large eagles. It prefers trees of the open (1) ______________ country, generally avoiding thick jungle. Eagles often (2) ______________ high on trees or poles. It is (3) ______________ on the Nullarbor Plains and can be seen in (4) ______________ by train passengers crossing the desert.

The (5) ______________ builds its nest with a good view of the countryside. The nest may be built in either a live or dead tree, but usually the tallest one in the territory. In parts of Australia, where tall trees are absent, small trees, cliff faces or even the ground may be used.

The nest is large and made of dead sticks. The chicks get their first (6) ______________ during the second week after hatching.

The Wedge-tailed Eagle is Australia's largest living bird of (7) ______________ and one of the largest eagles in the world.

Tricky words

The words ***prey*** and ***pray*** sound the same but have different spellings. Words that sound the same but have different spellings are called **homophones**.

Word	Meaning	Example
prey	animals that are caught, killed and eaten by other animals	*Fish are **prey** for sea eagles.*
pray	1 speak to a god or saint	*At church, the priest will **pray** for help.*
	2 hope for something strongly	*I **pray** that it won't rain on Saturday.*

Complete the following sentences with the correct word (*ate* or *eight*).

1. Some people get down on their knees to ____________________.
2. The lion followed its ____________________ across the grassy plains.
3. Many people ____________________ in their place of worship.
4. The wren became ____________________ to a native cat.
5. Draw a line from each hunter below to its prey.

frog	mouse
lion	fly
snake	deer

Looking at … *wr* words

Many words start with ***wr***. The ***w*** in these words is usually silent, e.g. ***wr****ap*, ***wr****ong*, ***wr****ing*, ***wr****inkle*. Write the full ***wr*** words below.

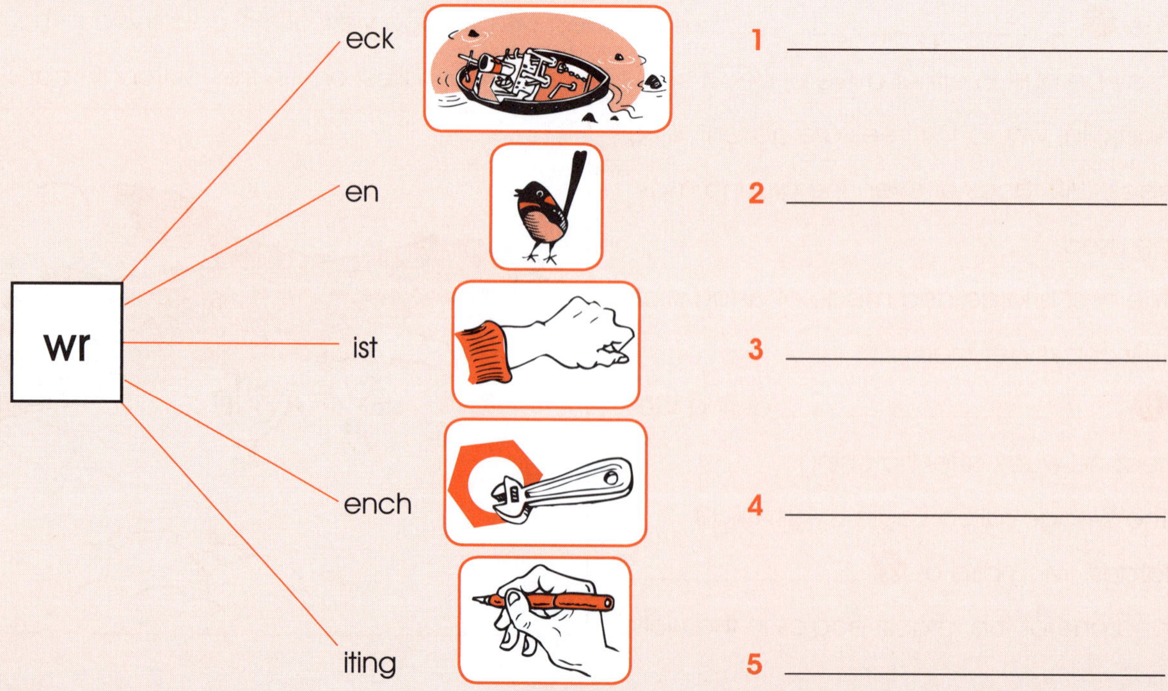

Proofreading

Circle the six mistakes and write the words correctly above them.

The Australian emu is the world's second tallest bird. It is flightles and often wanders in large herds across the open planes where it is quite comon. Here it can do great damage where crops can be flattened. However, the bird has its good points. It may eat plant food but it also prays on grubs and insects including grasshoppers, which can wipe out hole crops over night.

The emu nests on the ground and lays about ten eggs. It is the male that sits on the nest to hatch the eggs. This takes about eight weeks.

It is a shy but inquisitive bird and when scared it will run, reaching speeds of 50 km/h in short bursts. It avoids forrests. The emu is protected in most areas.

Vocabulary power

Over the years many words take on new meanings. Let's look at some **idioms** and **proverbs** using **birds**. What do you mean when you call someone a *parrot*? Usually you mean they repeat the words of others. If you call someone a *galah*, you probably mean that they are being silly. Not very nice!

What do these terms below mean? Write a short explanation for each.

1. the early bird catches the worm ____________________
2. a bird's eye view ____________________
3. birds of a feather flock together ____________________
4. birdwatcher ____________________
5. a bit of a bower bird ____________________

Did you know?

There is a place in outback South Australia called Birdsville.

Read and learn

Work out the meanings of the words in **bold** by using the context.

A really **eye-catching** sight is a huge flock of warm pink and silvery grey galahs. What a spectacle to see them **wheeling** through the air against a blue sky! Then suddenly they **alight** in fields of wheat or like a mass of blossom in trees.

Galahs are one of the most common of the parrots found in all parts of Australia, although they prefer open country. They feed on seeds, grain, fruit, blossom and shoots, as well as some insects.

They are often **observed** in pairs as well as large flocks. Many have come to live close to towns and many suburbs in the cities are visited by galahs. The calls of the galahs are extremely **diverse**, ranging from loud whistles to shrieks and screams.

Circle the answers **a**, **b** or **c** that mean almost the same as the words in **bold** above.

1. eye-catching **a** sudden **b** harmful **c** dazzling
2. wheeling **a** rolling **b** turning **c** spinning
3. alight **a** land **b** leave **c** flutter
4. observed **a** caught **b** seen **c** contained
5. diverse **a** dive **b** tuneful **c** varied

Puzzle

How many of the words from the **Topic spelling list** can you write **across** the word ***honeyeater***? Only put one letter in each box and don't use the same word more than once.

				H				
				O				
				N				
				E				
				Y				
				E				
				A				
				T				
				E				
				R				

Your turn to write

Imagine you are a small bird, such as a canary or a budgie, and you have just escaped from a cage. Write your adventure in the 'first person'—that is, you must **pretend to be** the bird. You will need to use the word ***I*** often.

Tell of your adventures as you learn to survive in the bush. What are the dangers? How do you keep safe? How do you find food or water? Who are your enemies? Do you wish you hadn't escaped?

At the end of your story, draw a picture either in the cage or in the wilds. When you have revised your story, you can make a published copy.

Reading for fun

A policeman saw a man walking a penguin down the street. He told the man he should take the penguin to the zoo.

'Good idea', the man replied, and off he went.

The next day the policeman saw the man again, and he still had the penguin with him. 'I thought I told you to take that penguin to the zoo.'

'I did,' the man replied. 'Today I'm taking him to the movies.'

Q What do you call a slim parrot?

A Poly-unsaturated!

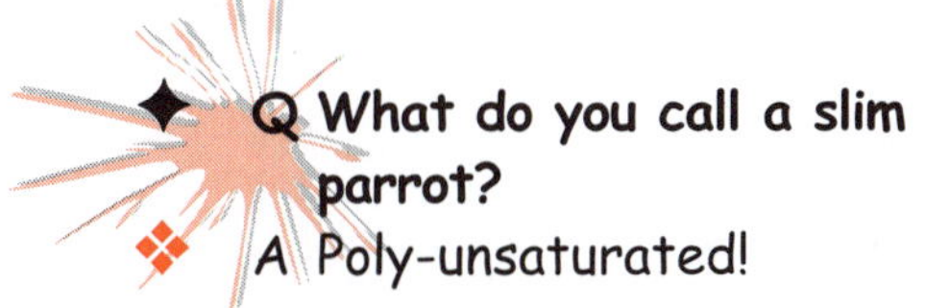

Q What do you get if you cross a budgie with a woodpecker?

A A bird that talks in Morse Code!

☞Answers on page 113

15 It's about time!

Quick fun

1. Arrange the words in the box from shortest in time to longest. Write them on the line below.

minute	second	fortnight	day
month	hour	year	

____

____

2. What is the opposite of *departure*? ____________________

3. Name the following.

a 

b 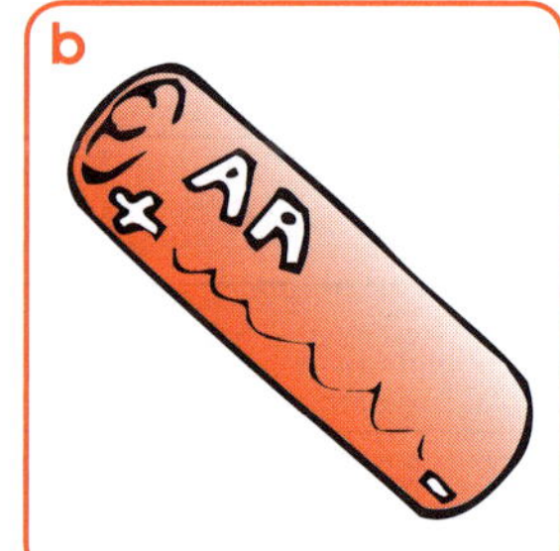

c 

____________ ____________ ____________

Topic spelling list

Use the **LOOK-SAY-COVER-WRITE-CHECK** strategy to learn these words.

minute	waiting	daily
hourly	arrival	month
weekly	queue	winder
second	timetable	fortnight
departure	sweep	yearly
during	watch	battery

Use this space to write out your topic words the first time. Use your own paper for extra practice.

Rewrite here those you had most trouble with.

Spelling strategy

Letter patterns: *ue* words

a queue

In many words, the letters ***ue*** rhyme with *you* or *two*.
The word ***queue*** has a strange spelling but it also rhymes with *you* or *two*.
A ***queue*** is a line of people waiting for something.
A ***cue*** is a stick for striking snooker balls. It sounds the same as *queue*.

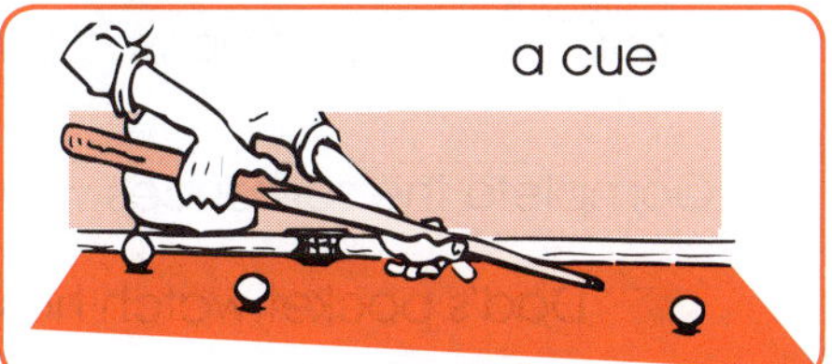
a cue

1 How many words do you know that rhyme with *blue* and have ***ue*** in them? Write your words here. The first letters have been done for you.

a S ____________ **b** BL ____________ **c** TR ____________ **d** CL ____________

e D ____________ **f** GL ____________ **g** ARG ____________

A ***revue*** is an amusing stage show.
A ***venue*** is the place where an event is held.

2 What is the missing ***ue*** word?
The detective is looking for a ____________.

Fill in the gaps

Complete the gaps with these words from the **Topic spelling list**.

second battery during winder watch waiting

A stopwatch is used to show how long an event has taken. To start and stop the (1) ____________, the user presses a button. By pressing the button again the time taken is shown. In many competitions, fractions of a (2) ____________ are shown.

Mechanical stopwatches have a (3) ____________ attached to a mainspring. Such watches must be wound up by turning the knob at the top of the watch. Digital stopwatches, which are powered by a (4) ____________, are much more accurate than mechanical timepieces.

Stopwatches are used by timekeepers to measure time taken (5) ____________ an event. Many stopwatches are connected to large screens. There is no (6) ____________ while the timekeepers work out the fastest finishers and their times in competitions.

Tricky words

The words ***hour*** and ***our*** sound the same but have different spellings. Words that sound the same but have different spellings are called **homophones**.

Word	Meaning	Example
hour	(silent ***h***) time: 60 minutes	*I'll be one **hour** late.*
our	people who own something	***Our** class won the award.*

Complete the sentences with the correct word (*hour* or *our*).

1. Dad's pocket watch has a winder but ________________ watches have batteries.
2. 'Give me half an ________________ to get ready,' called Sophie.
3. ________________ family won the trip to Fiji.
4. What is best for showing one minute has passed? (*tick one*)

   stopwatch ☐ calendar ☐ timetable ☐

5. Complete this table.

60	________________	=	1 minute
60	________________	=	1 hour
14 days		=	a ________________
24	________________	=	1 day

Looking at … revision of plurals

You have been shown how to make plurals in earlier lessons.

1. Can you complete this table?

One	More than one	One	More than one
1 second		2 battery	
3 minute		4 watch	
5 month		6 queue	
7 winder		8 arrival	
9 timetable		10 departure	

Did you know?

The word *fortnight* comes from the old English—fourteen nights.

Proofreading

Circle the seven mistakes and write the words correctly in the box below.

A sundial is a device that measures time by the position of the Sun. The most commonly sean designs, such as the 'ordinary' garden sundial, cast a shadow on a flat surface marked with the ours of the day. As the position of the sun changes, the time shown by the shadow changes. However, sundials can be designed for any surface where the sun casts a shadow.

It would be hard to wear a sundial on your rist as a wristwatch or put it into a pocket as a pocket watch. It would hardly work with a timetabel in underground railway stations, or on a rainy day anywhere.

The oldest sundial in Britain is divided into four tides, representing the parts of the working day. This was well before clockwork watchs with windars became common. However, a sundial is of little use in telling the day of the week or the mounth of the year.

One of the world's most famous clocks is Big Ben in London.

Vocabulary power

We know words can have more than one meaning. Let's look at ***second***. It can mean:

a a small amount of time (There are 60 seconds in a minute.)
b the next position after first.

Can you find the words from the **Topic spelling list** that have all the following meanings?

1. **a** look at something
   b a device for keeping time
   c a period when a guard is on duty

   The word is ______________________.

2. **a** use a broom
   b the name of the second hand of a watch that does a full circle of the face
   c a detailed search

   The word is ______________________.

3. **a** a grouping of similar objects
   b a store for electrical power

   The word is ______________________.

Read and learn

Use the context clues to work out the meanings of the words in **bold**.

Timetables have many forms and uses. Railway timetables may be printed in the form of **brochures** or books, or on notice boards consisting of tables that **indicate** the **schedule** times of arrival and departure at stations along one or more railway routes. Most timetables are now available on the Internet.

A student's school timetable may be a single page in a homework diary. It will **inform** students where and when their **specific** classes will be held. In some schools, some classes are located in laboratories or music rooms or art rooms. A timetable will tell students which room they have been assigned for each class.

Circle the answers **a**, **b** or **c** that mean almost the same as the words in **bold** above.

1. brochures — **a** newspapers — **b** leaflets — **c** mail
2. indicate — **a** show — **b** deliver — **c** lights
3. scheduled — **a** arrival — **b** planned — **c** starting
4. inform — **a** report — **b** measure — **c** advise
5. specific — **a** particular — **b** listed — **c** student

Puzzle

Find one word from the **Topic spelling list** for each row. Write your answers **across** the grid. Some of the letters for each word are already in place. When you have completed the grid, unscramble the letters down the centre column to make one of the words from the **Topic spelling list**. It is not always the first and last letters that are given.

		D				Y				
					O	N		H		
W			K		Y					
Q		E	U							
						T	T			
			W		T		H			
M			U		E					
		W	E		P					
	W		I		I		G			

Write your unscrambled word here.

____

Your turn to write

You have just arrived home late from visiting a friend. Your father or mother greets you with, 'It's about time!'

Explain why you are late. You can invent an amusing reason if you like.

Use some of the words from the **Topic spelling list**. At the end of your story, draw a picture of what you were really doing when you should have been home!

When you have revised your story, you can make a published copy.

It's about time!

Q Why did the fool have his sundial lit!

A So he could tell the time at night!

Doctor, Doctor! I feel like a snooker ball!

Please wait your turn and go to the end of the queue!

☞Answers on pages 113–114

Review 3

Now let's see what you remember of the words you learnt in Units 5–10. There are four tests in this review. You could do all in one session, or you could break them up and do them over a few days.

Step 1 Look at each group of words in the test to revise the spellings.

Step 2 Cover the five words up and test yourself (column 2). Try to do all five words in one go.

Step 3 Write your score out of 5 in the box. If you got any words wrong, go back and study them again.

Step 4 If possible, ask someone to test you on the words later—an hour or even a day later (column 3).

Test 1

Study	Test yourself	Test with another person
twenty dozen waterless submarine answer	/5	/5
watery whisper softly magpie wren	/5	/5
rare minute hourly four thirty	/5	/5
	Total score = out of 15	Total score = out of 15

Test 2

Study	Test yourself	Test with another person
total drought argue sigh tongue	/5	/5
flight galah perch second departing	/5	/5
during seven forty downpour tanker	/5	/5
daily month winder twelve fourteen	/5	/5
	Total score = out of 20	Total score = out of 20

Test 3

Study	Test yourself	Test with another person
rower reply language feathers nectar	/5	/5
waiting arrival queue eight fifty	/5	/5
century canoe surface submerge discuss	/5	/5
number skiing sailor silent thought		
	Total score = out of 20	Total score = out of 20

Test 4

Study	Test yourself	Test with another person
question slang eagle brightly timetable	/5	/5
eleven hundred kayak float captain	/5	/5
discussion laugh parrot forest ringing	/5	/5
	Total score = out of 15	Total score = out of 15

Which word?

1. There were ______________ and twenty blackbirds baked in a pie. (*for, four*)
2. We watched the ______________ race on Sydney harbour. (*ferry, fairy*)
3. 'I can't eat this meat,' said Mum. 'It's ______________.' (*roar, raw*)
4. Many people prefer to ______________ where there is peace and quiet. (*prey, pray*)

☞Answers on page 114

Word list

actor
after
alps
ankle
answer
arena
argue
arrival
arrive
artist
asleep
baker
bakery
bandicoot
bank
banker
barber
bare
bark
basketball
battery
beach
beak
bear
birds
blew
blue

bone
books
bought
brain
branches
brightly
brought
builder
bus
bushfire
butcher
butterfingers
buy
by
cafe
cage
calf
camel
canoe
captain
cash
cattle
century
cheers
chemist
chest
city

clothes
clue
coach
colourless
common
complete
count
country
course
crawl
cricket
crop
crowd
daily
dear
deer
dentist
depart
departure
destroy
direct
dirty
discuss
discussion
distance
doctor
dogs

downpour
dozen
draw
driver
drought
due
during
dwarf
each
eagle
ear
earn
earth
east
eat
eight
elephant
eleven
elf
energy
estimate
exam
explore
eyes
fair
fairly
fairy

fare
farm
farmer
farmhouse
farmyard
father
fearless
feathers
feed
feet
fence
ferry
field
fifty
finger
fingerling
fireman
firewood
first
flight
float
flock
flour
flower
food
for
forest
fortnight
forty
found
fountain
four
fourteen
freestyle
friend
frosty
fruit
fuel
gaggle
galah
gentleman
ghost
giant
giggle
glue
gnome
goal
grass
grassy
green
greengrocer
ground
guard
gumleaf
gym
hair
hairdresser
happily
happy
harpist
harvest
hatless
health
healthy
heart
herd
highway
hips
hole
holiday
honeyeater
hopefully
hound
hour
hourly
human
hundred
incomplete
indirect
inhuman
insane
insects
invisible
journey
kayak
king
kiosk
knuckle
koala
lab
lake
language
laugh
lead
leaf
lean
leaves
light
lion
litter
lonely
magic
magician
magpie
main
marine
market
meat
milk
milky
minute
monkey
month
motor
mound
mount
mountain
mouth
music
musician

nearly
neck
nectar
nerve
nesting
netball
newsagent
newspaper
night
novelist
number
numeral
nurse
ocean
once
organist
ouch
our
out
oval
pack
panda
parents
parrot
path
perch
picnic
pigpen
pigs
pixie
place
plain
plane
planet
planting
player
playing
plumber
pod
pointless
policeman
pound
prey
pride
prince
princess
queen
question
queue
quickly
railway
rare
raw
red
reply
reptile
revue
right
ringing
rink
river
roads
roar
round
rower
sadly
sailor
sandy
sane
scarecrow
scared
school
scoreless
seashore
seats
second
seven
shed
sheep
shell
shoes
shop
shopping
sigh
sight
silent
skiing
slang
slowly
smile
snowy
soccer
socks
softly
solar
soloist
sound
speechless
speed
spell
sport
stadium
stamps
starter
starting
station
storeroom
stream
street
subhuman
submarine
submerge
subsoil
subsonic
subtitle
sue
sugar
suitcase
supermarket
supersonic

surface
swarm
sweep
swimming
tale
tanker
taxi
teacher
think
thirty
thorny
thought
three
ticket
tiger
time
timetable
told
toll
tongue
total
tour
tourist
town
tractor
train
travel
traveller
troll
troop
true
twelve
twenty
ugly
useless
valley
venue
vet
visible
visit
visitor
waiting
warble
watch
waterless
watery
weekly
well
whale
what
wheat
wheel
wheelchair
whip
whisper
whistle
whole
winder
windmill
windy
winner
witch
wizard
wombat
woods
wool
working
wreck
wren
wrench
wrist
writing
yearly
young

Answers

1 Let's go shopping (pages 2–7)

Quick fun (page 2)
1 BANK **2** BAKERY **3** FOOD **4** BOOKS **5** SHOP **6** SUPERMARKET

Spelling strategy (page 3)
1 bakry ✗ (bakery) **2** butcher ✓ **3** shose ✗ (shoes) **4** mete ✗ (meat)

Fill in the gaps (page 3)
1 bank, cash **2** shops **3** fruit **4** meat **5** stamps
6 newspaper **7** socks

Tricky words (page 4)
1 brought, brought **2** brought **3** bought **4** bought **5** brought

Proofreading (page 5)
shopping, chemist, clothes, butchers, bakery, eight

Vocabulary power (page 5)
1 hairdresser **2** newspapers **3** suitcase **4** classroom
5 newsagent **6** greengrocer **7** wheelchair **8** haystack
9 scarecrow **10** bushfire

Read and learn (page 6)
1 a **2** b **3** a **4** c **5** b

Puzzle (page 6)

B	A	K	E	R	Y	N	C	O	C
U	A	E	A	S	Z	Y	L	D	P
T	R	G	I	X	S	H	O	E	S
C	H	E	M	I	S	T	T	B	O
H	J	G	M	I	L	F	H	O	C
E	F	F	E	B	C	O	E	O	K
R	T	B	L	D	B	O	S	K	S
U	H	B	R	E	A	D	G	S	Q
F	R	U	I	T	N	W	I	J	X
V	K	M	I	L	K	C	A	S	H

1 fruit **2** meat

2 Lend a hand (pages 8–13)

Quick fun (page 8)
Suggested answers: CAN, CANS, MUSIC, SCAN, SUM, AS, US, IS, AM, AN, MAN, SCUM, SIN, MAIN, AIM, MINI.
The eight-letter word is MUSICIAN.

Spelling strategy (page 9)

1 sky

2 **a** all **b** egg 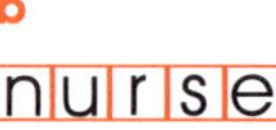

3 **a** actor **b** nurse **c** plumber 

Fill in the gaps (pages 9–10)
1 **a** doctor, nurse **b** fireman **c** barber, hairdresser **d** parents **e** musician **f** teacher **g** dentist **h** policeman **i** actor
2 **a** fireman **b** policeman **c** plumber **d** hairdresser **e** musician
3 a bank
4 musician (*flautist* is the specific name for a person who plays the flute)

Tricky words (page 10)
1 blew **2** blew **3** blue **4** blue

Vocabulary power (page 10)
1 invisible **2** indirect **3** insane **4** incomplete **5** inhuman

Looking at … plurals: adding *s* (page 11)
1 cats **2** seats **3** books **4** bakers **5** houses **6** nurses
7 actors **8** plumbers

Proofreading (page 11)
shopping, barber, milk, water, fruit, stamps

Read and learn (page 12)
1 a **2** b **3** b **4** c **5** b **6** c

Puzzle (pages 12–13)
1 **a** DOCTOR **b** DENTIST **c** BAKER **d** PLUMBER **e** NURSE **f** POLICEMAN
2 **a** FRIEND **b** MUSICIAN **c** ARTIST **d** FIREMAN **e** BUILDER

3 A walk in the park (pages 14–19)

Quick fun (page 14)
1 rats **2** net **3** nib **4** nap **5** music **6** cafe **7** lake **8** bark

Spelling strategy (page 15)
1 **a** SEAT **b** HEAT **c** TREAT **d** WHEAT **e** BEAT **f** NEAT **g** MEAT **h** REPEAT
2 east

Fill in the gaps (page 15)
1 music **2** visitors **3** flowers **4** dogs **5** seats **6** lake **7** birds **8** tree **9** leaves **10** branches **11** insects **12** park

Tricky words (page 16)
1 break **2** break **3** brake **4** break **5** brake **6** brake **7** break

Looking at ... plurals: adding es to words ending in *ch* and *sh* (page 16)
1 branches **2** splashes **3** bunches **4** crashes **5** lunches **6** patches

Proofreading (page 17)
1 path, grass, two, leaves, branches
2 **a** dogs ✓ **b** brids ✗ (birds) **c** insecks ✗ (insects) **d** picnick ✗ (picnic) **e** cafe ✓

Vocabulary power (page 17)
1 park **2** seat(s) **3** green

Read and learn (page 18)
1 c **2** b **3** a **4** b **5** a

Puzzle (page 18)
kael—lake, kkois—kiosk, ranchbes—branches, nurtk— trunk, eatss—seats, rassg—grass, aeelvs—leaves, karb—bark, rostsiiv—visitors, hapt—path

4 Once upon a time (pages 20–25)

Quick fun (page 20)
1 **a** princess **b** giant **c** magician **d** elf **e** ghost **f** fairy
2 a fairy tale

Spelling strategy (page 21)
Suggested answers: sell, tell, dell, dwell, bell, fell, swell, yell

Fill in the gaps (page 21)
1 time **2** king **3** princess **4** prince **5** queen **6** woods **7** giant **8** love **9** happily **10** after

Tricky words (page 22)
1 buy **2** by **3** buy **4** by **5** By **6** by

Looking at ... plurals: words ending in *f* (page 22)
1 wharves **2** hooves **3** calves **4** halves **5** leaves **6** scarves

Proofreading (page 23)
witch, happily, ate, grass, magic, prince

Vocabulary power (page 23)
Suggested answers: **1** wicked wizard **2** mean witch **3** white ghost **4** angry giant **5** yellow leaf **6** baby bird **7** huge truck **8** pretty dress

Read and learn (page 24)
1 b **2** a **3** c **4** c **5** b

Puzzle (page 24)
Suggested answers:
1 Few wizards sell little elf frogs.
2 Big ghosts steal little eggs.

5 What about me? (pages 26–31)

Quick fun (page 26)
1 neck **2** hip **3** ankle **4** feet **5** calf **6** knuckle **7** mouth **8** hair

Fill in the gaps (page 27)
1 hair **2** heart **3** bone **4** hip **5** medicine **6** energy **7** nerves **8** health

Tricky words (page 28)
1 dear **2** deer **3** dear **4** deer

Looking at ... plurals: adding es to words ending in *s*, *x* or *z* (page 28)
1 **a** boxes **b** classes **c** mixes **d** buzzes **e** buses **f** passes
2 **a** sixes **b** tosses

Proofreading (page 29)
to, chest, bones, knuckles, fingers, heart, right

Vocabulary power (page 29)
1 young fish about the size of a finger **2** food eaten with the fingers **3** unwilling to help out in any way **4** close by **5** just missed out on catching something **6** can't hold or catch anything without dropping it

Read and learn (page 30)
1 in a pack of cards **2** when a person loses someone dear to him/her
Suggested answers: heartthrob, sweetheart, heartwarming, heartening, heartfelt, heartburn

Puzzle (page 30)

1 dear **2** hips **3** deer **4** feet **5** heart **6** smile, miles **7** heart **8** nerve

Review 1 (pages 32–35)

Which word? (page 35)

1 ate **2** blew **3** break **4** buy **5** deer

6 On the farm (pages 36–41)

Quick fun (page 36)

1 windmill **2** sheep **3** wheat **4** shed **5** scarecrow **6** fence **7** wool **8** farmhouse **9** pigs **10** tractor

Spelling strategy (page 37)

1 market, harvest, farm, farmer, farmhouse, scarecrow
2 Suggested answers: bark, dark, hark, lark, park

Fill in the gaps (page 37)

1 farmer **2** windmill **3** cattle, pigs, sheep **4** harvest **5** feed **6** farmhouse **7** planting **8** tractor

Tricky words (page 38)

1 flower **2** flower **3** flour **4** flour

Looking at ... non-changing plurals (page 38)

1 glasses **2** pants **3** scissors **4** salmon **5** starfish

Proofreading (page 39)

tracter ✗ (tractor), sheep ✓, windmil ✓, fence ✓, scarcrow ✗ (scarecrow), shed ✓, fermer ✗ (farmer), cattel ✗ (cattle), wheet ✗ (wheat)

Vocabulary power (page 39)

1 pig + pen **2** farm + yard **3** gum + leaf **4** scarecrow, windmill, farmhouse **5** gentleman, firewood, railway, highway, storeroom (5)

Read and learn (page 40)

1 a **2** c **3** b **4** a **5** b

Puzzle (page 40)

1			**F**	A	R	M		
2		C	**A**	T	T	L	E	
3	H	A	**R**	V	E	S	T	
4			**M**	A	R	K	E	T
5		F	**E**	N	C	E		
6		T	**R**	A	C	T	O	R

7 Travelling on (pages 42–47)

Quick fun (page 42)

1. Did you arrive before the train?
2. The guard was not at the station.
3. We depart for our holiday on Sunday.
4. We got to the toll road and had to pay.

Spelling strategy (page 43)

1 train, main
2 a MAIN **b** RAIN **c** TRAIN **d** PLAIN **e** GAIN **f** GRAIN **g** DRAIN **h** PAIN

Fill in the gaps (page 43)

1 travel **2** street **3** journey **4** crowd **5** ticket **6** rain

Tricky words (page 44)

1 fare, fare **2** fair **3** fair **4** fare **5** fair

Looking at ... plurals as new words (page 44)

1 geese **2** feet **3** children **4** women

Proofreading (page 45)

rain, arrived, friend, teacher, mouth, lake, crowd

Vocabulary power (page 45)

1 soloist **2** artist **3** organist **4** novelist

Read and learn (page 46)

1 b **2** a **3** c **4** b **5** a

Puzzle (page 46)

R	O	A	D	S		
A	R	R	I	V	E	
T	I	C	K	E	T	
D	E	P	A	R	T	
T	R	A	V	E	L	
T	O	U	R	I	S	T

1 STREET

2 crowd

8 Be a sport (pages 48–53)

Quick fun (page 48)

1 goal **2** whistle **3** cricket **4** netball **5** swimming **6** oval

Spelling strategy (page 49)

1 marking **2** racing **3** scoring **4** cheering **5** playing **6** changing **7** firing **8** bowling **9** forming **10** using

Fill in the gaps (page 49)

1 oval **2** player **3** soccer **4** draw **5** winner **6** distance **7** place **8** speed **9** goal **10** cricket **11** swimming **12** train

Tricky words (page 50)

1 whole **2** hole **3** whole **4** hole **5** whole

Looking at … *wh* words (page 50)

1 whistle **2** whip **3** whale **4** what **5** wheel

Proofreading (page 51)

oval, train, soccer, netball, parents, park

Vocabulary power (page 51)

Suggested answers: swimming, diving, water polo

Read and learn (page 52)

1 a **2** b **3** a **4** c **5** c **6** b

Puzzle (page 52)

1 NETBALL **2** WINNER **3** DISTANCE **4** STARTER

9 To the zoo (pages 54–59)

Quick fun (page 54)

1 **a** lion **b** monkey **c** koala **d** panda **e** elephant **f** bandicoot **g** tiger **h** bear **i** camel **j** wombat

2 cats

Spelling strategy (page 55)

1 hissed **2** nursed **3** growled **4** barked **5** dived **6** acted **7** whistle **8** used **9** banked **10** glided

Fill in the gaps (page 55)

1 **a** visit **b** camel **c** bear **d** lizard **e** reptile **f** asleep **g** scared **h** healthy

2 **a** tiger **b** elephant **c** wombat **d** camel **e** bandicoot

3 koala, bandicoot, wombat

Tricky words (page 56)

1 bear **2** bare **3** bare **4** bare **5** bare **6** bear

Looking at … alliteration (page 56)

Suggested answers:

1 **a** wobbly wombat **b** lazy lizard **c** brown bear **d** tired tortoise **e** crazy cricket **f** hungry horse

2 **a** toothless tiger **b** fat frog **c** dangerous dog

Proofreading (page 57)

bare, seats, parents, to, visit, shopping, buy

Vocabulary power (page 57)

1 mice, locusts, insects **2** ants, seagulls **3** hens **4** insects, mosquitoes

Read and learn (page 58)

1 b **2** b **3** c **4** a **5** a

Puzzle (page 58)

T	T	I	G	E	R	Y	B	E	A	R	E
H	P	Q	K	O	A	L	A	L	T	Q	I
B	J	V	A	J	P	U	N	E	Z	F	D
L	I	O	N	N	E	E	D	P	F	C	R
L	C	I	G	W	Q	X	I	H	X	A	F
I	P	A	A	L	B	G	C	A	M	M	H
Z	E	B	R	A	K	M	O	N	K	E	Y
A	U	D	O	C	E	R	O	T	G	L	N
R	B	W	O	M	B	A	T	E	M	L	S
D	K	V	D	G	S	T	O	M	D	H	P
C	A	Z	L	W	P	A	N	D	A	Y	O

10 Our world (pages 60–65)

Quick fun (page 60)

1 Your back will **be ach**ing by tonight (beach)

2 It is a cro**w or king** parrot in the tree! (working)

3 Do trucks **tow n**ew cars away? (town)

4 Can Paul **count rye** seeds on his plate? (country)

Spelling strategy (page 61)

1 mountain, country

2 **a** BOUT **b** ABOUT **c** TROUT **d** POUT **e** LOUT **f** STOUT **g** SPOUT

3 south

Fill in the gaps (page 61)

1 **a** explore **b** stream **c** river **d** valley **e** ocean **f** beach **g** forest **h** country **i** town.

2 alps

3 city

4 forest

Tricky words (pages 61–62)

1 plane **2** plane **3** plain **4** plain **5** plain **6** plane

Looking at … shortened words (page 62)

1 **a** **exam**ination **b** **lab**oratory **c** omni**bus** **d** **taxi**cab **e** **vet**erinary **f** **gym**nasium

2 **a** submarine **b** telephone **c** utility

Proofreading (page 63)

I love a sunburnt (countery)	country
A land of sweeping (planes)	plains
Of ragged (montain) ranges,	mountain
(Off) droughts and flooding rains	of
I love her far horizons,	✓
I love her jewel (see)	sea
Her beauty (an) her terror	and
The wide brown land (four) me!	for

Vocabulary power (page 63)
1 plain **2** earth **3** stream

Read and learn (page 64)
1 a **2** c **3** b **4** c

Puzzle (page 64)
Suggested answers:
1 at, mat, hem, them, tic, tics, he
2 scare, scar, care, car, are, crow, row

Review 2 (pages 66–69)

Which word? (page 69)
1 flour **2** fare **3** hole **4** bare **5** plain

11 What's your number? (pages 70–75)

Quick fun (page 70)
two, three, four, seven, eight, right

Spelling strategy (page 71)
1 **a** 2 **b** 12 **c** 2 **d** 20 **e** 2
2 **a** eight **b** forty **c** fourteen **d** twelve **e** twenty-four

Fill in the gaps (page 71)
two, Three, four, Seven, eight, Eleven, twelve, fourteen, twenty

Tricky words (page 72)
1 forty **2** four **3** for **4** for **5** Four
6 **a** forty-four **b** four **c** forty **d** fourteen

Proofreading (page 72)
friend, two, sea, four, four, for

Looking at … plurals: words ending in *y* (page 73)
1 **a** bays **b** days **c** ladies **d** berries **e** worries **f** cities
2 **a** centuries **b** twenties

Vocabulary power (page 73)
number one—myself, me; on cloud nine—very happy; put two and two together—work something out; two's company, three's a crowd—two people together are okay, but three people together cause problems; forty winks—a short sleep; dressed to the nines—dressed very nicely; the one and only—something special; there is only one of something; six of one and half a dozen of the other—it's the same thing

Read and learn (page 74)
1 a **2** c **3** b **4** b

12 Water, water (pages 76–81)

Quick fun (page 76)
1 SAILOR **2** WATERY **3** CAPTAIN **4** SUBMERGE **5** FREESTYLE **6** CANOE **7** ROWER **8** TANKER **9** SURFACE **10** DROUGHT **11** *Titanic*

Spelling strategy (page 77)
1 dirty **2** grassy **3** sandy **4** milky **5** thorny **6** snowy **7** windy **8** frosty **9** Frosty

Fill in the gaps (page 77)
1 **a** drought **b** captain **c** submarine **d** rower **e** freestyle **f** ferry **g** tanker **h** waterless
2 **a** skiing **b** canoe **c** sailor **d** kayak

Tricky words (page 78)
1 ferry **2** fairy **3** ferry **4** fairy **5** ferry

Proofreading (page 78)
sailor, downpour, skiing, waterless, marine, surface, submerge (seven)

Looking at … palindromes (page 79)
1 eye
2 **a** NOON **b** LEVEL **c** EWE **d** MUM
3 dad, did, dud; pap, pep, pip, pop, pup; gag, gig; wow

Vocabulary power (page 79)
1 subway **2** subtitle **3** subsoil **4** subsonic **5** subhuman

Read and learn (page 80)
1 a **2** b **3** c **4** a **5** c

Puzzle (page 80)
1 **a** FERRY **b** CAPTAIN **c** DROUGHT **d** KAYAK **e** WATERY **f** SKIING **g** ROWER **h** MARINE
2 **a** 19, 21, 2, 13, 1, 18, 9, 14, 5
b 4, 15, 23, 14, 16, 15, 21, 18

13 What did you say? (pages 82–87)

Quick fun (page 82)

1 whisper **2** reply **3** discuss **4** giggle **5** laugh

Spelling strategy (page 83)

1 right, right **2** right **3** tight **4** high **5** sigh

Fill in the gaps (page 83)

1 giggle **2** whisper **3** question, answer **4** discussion
5 thought **6** language **7** tongue **8** slang **9** Answers will vary

Tricky words (page 84)

1 **a** raw **b** roar **c** roar **d** raw
2 tiger, lion

Looking at … adverbs with *ly* (page 84)

1 Slowly, quietly, soundly, Carefully, gently, completely
2 **a** sadly **b** quickly **c** neatly **d** Hopefully **e** slowly

Proofreading (page 85)

roared, giant, branches, flowers, when, slipped

Vocabulary power (page 85)

1 pointless **2** scoreless **3** fearless **4** colourless **5** useless
6 hatless

Read and learn (page 86)

1 b **2** b **3** c **4** a **5** c

Puzzle (page 86)

Suggested answers:

a	asked	**b**	boasted	**c**	called
d	demanded	**e**	explained	**f**	fumed
g	guessed	**h**	howled	**i**	interrupted
j	joked	**k**	kidded	**l**	lied
m	moaned	**n**	noted	**o**	objected
p	pleaded	**q**	questioned	**r**	roared
s	stammered	**t**	teased	**u**	uttered
v	ventured	**w**	wailed	**x**	
y	yelled	**z**			

14 For the birds (pages 88–93)

Quick fun (page 88)

1 Dee**r are** eaten by lions. (rare)
2 'A pro**per ch**ain won't break!' called Dad. (perch)
3 The **feat her s**ister performed was amazing. (feathers)
4 Can we b**ring in g**roups of twelve? (ringing)
5 Always switch of**f light**s when you leave the room! (flight)

Spelling strategy (page 89)

1 nectar **2** father **3** soccer **4** actor **5** motor **6** solar **7** sugar
8 visitor

Fill in the gaps (page 89)

1 forest **2** perch **3** common **4** flight **5** eagle **6** feathers **7** prey

Tricky words (page 90)

1 pray **2** prey **3** pray **4** prey **5** frog–fly, lion–deer, snake–mouse

Looking at … *wr* words (page 90)

1 wreck **2** wren **3** wrist **4** wrench **5** writing

Proofreading (page 91)

flightless, plains, common, preys, whole, forests

Vocabulary power (page 91)

1 first come first served
2 as seen from above
3 your reputation will be the same as the people you go around with
4 a person who enjoys studying birds in their habitat
5 a person who collects things

Read and learn (page 92)

1 c **2** b **3** a **4** b **5** c

Puzzle (page 92)

Suggested answers:

F	E	A	T	**H**	E	R	S		
			C	**O**	M	M	O	N	
	W	R	E	**N**					
	F	O	R	**E**	S	T			
	P	R	E	**Y**					
				E	A	G	L	E	
			W	**A**	R	B	L	E	
	N	E	C	**T**	A	R			
			P	**E**	R	C	H		
				R	A	R	E		

15 It's about time (pages 94–99)

Quick fun (page 94)

1 second, minute, hour, day, fortnight, month, year
2 arrival
3 **a** watch **b** battery **c** queue

Spelling strategy (page 95)

1 **a** SUE **b** BLUE **c** TRUE **d** CLUE **e** DUE **f** GLUE **g** ARGUE

2 clue

Fill in the gaps (page 95)

1 watch **2** second **3** winder **4** battery **5** during **6** waiting

Tricky words (page 96)

1 our **2** hour **3** Our **4** stopwatch **5** 60 seconds = 1 minute; 60 minutes = 1 hour; 14 days = a fortnight; 24 hours = 1 day

Looking at ... revision of plurals (page 96)

1 seconds **2** batteries **3** minutes **4** watches **5** months **6** queues **7** winders **8** arrivals **9** timetables **10** departures

Proofreading (page 97)

seen, hours, wrist, timetable, watches, winders, month

Vocabulary power (page 97)

1 watch **2** sweep **3** battery

Read and learn (page 98)

1 b **2** a **3** b **4** c **5** a

Puzzle (page 98)

		D	A	**I**	L	Y				
				M	O	N	T	H		
W	E	E	K	**L**	Y					
Q	U	E	U	**E**						
				B	A	T	T	E	R	Y
			W	**A**	T	C	H			
M	I	N	U	**T**	E					
	S	W	E	**E**	P					
	W	A	I	**T**	I	N	G			

Unscrambled word = TIMETABLE

Review 3 (pages 100–103)

Which word? (page 103)

1 four **2** ferry **3** raw **4** pray

Notes

Notes